Psychology of School Learning

Psychology of School Learning

Paul E. Johnson
University of Minnesota

John Wiley & Sons, Inc. New York · London · Sydney · Toronto

6484

Preface

Psychology is frequently criticized because it has been relatively unsuccessful in providing a reliable foundation on which educational practice can be built. Certainly, the findings of psychology sometimes illuminate our understanding of specific patterns of behavior (for example, the use of operant conditioning principles in studying and treating behavioral pathology). More often, however, these findings seem remote from our everyday experience.

Nevertheless, this book is written from the point of view that knowledge of psychology can be of value to the practitioner, particularly when the problems of interest concern behavioral change or learning. This viewpoint rests on two assumptions about the relevance of theory for practice: (1) the practitioner has an intuitive but limited grasp of behavior, and his understanding of behavior is increased by seeing his own intuitions as instances of the more general behavioral models of psychology; and (2) the methods of psychology can be effectively employed by the practitioner in arranging conditions for behavioral change.

The book does not contain prescriptive statements for modifying behavior (these are properly found in a theory of instruction). Instead, the attempt is to rescue some of the phenomena of behavior from purely anecdotal illustration without resorting to citations of the experimental literature, the contents of which are usually regarded by the practitioner as being both irrelevant and trivial.

The book is short, partly because the interface between psychology and education is not easy to write about, and partly because of a belief that any attempt to relate theory and practice must draw heavily on the knowledge and intuitions of the individual instructor. The book is intended for advanced undergraduates in education and psychology and also for first-year graduate students in educational psychology. The annotated list of readings at the end of each chapter suggests ways in which individual topics can be pursued in depth depending on the instructor's purpose and the level of student competence.

Although final responsibility for the book is mine, I have profited from association with wise and talented people. Among them are Joseph F. Jordan, whose editorial acumen includes patiently waiting for manuscripts to be written; Paul W. Fox, whose virtues as a colleague include the art of gentle criticism; David Cox and Eugene Lenarz, who read the entire manuscript and saved it from many confusions; and Christine Miller who typed innumerable drafts.

My family deserves a special thanks for putting up with a preoccupied and occasionally downright annoying member of the household.

PAUL E. JOHNSON
June 1970

Contents

6484

Psychology of School Learning

1
Introduction

"Begin at the beginning," the King said, very gravely,
"and go on till you come to the end: then stop."

This book is written for the individual who attempts more or less systematically to change the behavior of others. Such individuals (for example, teachers, counselors, and trainers) usually make decisions about behavioral change based on their own intuition and their best judgment as to the determinants of the behaviors that confront them. Our primary goal is to provide a framework within which the science of psychology can be usefully related to everyday ideas for changing behavior.

The basic way to talk about behavioral change is through the term "learning." This term is used to describe phenomena from two points of view: the scientific and prescientific. A substantial portion of this book is concerned with the way in which learning is used in these two languages and how it can be usefully understood by those who are primarily concerned with practical situations.

The Concept of Learning

Within the science of psychology, learning has the status of a "construct." Constructs are ideas or images that cannot be directly observed, such as electrons and genes. What we do observe, however, are "dial readings" of one sort or another and, when certain patterns of readings appear (our measurements) we use these words to account for them.

We do not observe learning directly. Rather, for our understanding of learning we depend on a relationship between time and performance. More precisely, learning is defined in psychology as a relatively permanent change in behavior as a result of practice (some would say reinforced practice). To understand this definition, we would, of course, need some idea of how terms such as "practice" and "reinforcement" are used by the psychologist.

Let us simply say that the term learning, as well as the terms that define it, are based in a domain of activity (the science of experimental psychology) the primary concern of which is to describe and ultimately explain behavior. The goal of psychology is to understand the conditions under which certain well-defined behaviors are related to specific environmental events. As part of this activity, models and theories are constructed for the psychological processes of organisms whose behavior is being described. Within this framework, we say that we understand behavioral change when we can predict performance from a knowledge of environmental events.

The above orientation toward an understanding of learning is purely descriptive. Such an approach does not tell us what to do if we wish to change behavior in some specific way. From the point of view of the trainer or the teacher, the problem is usually how best to arrange the learning situation, that is, the sequence of activities or materials and the conditions of reward or punishment, so that the organism will learn some specific performance. How does this concern relate to what we know about learning from the psychological laboratory? This is an important and challenging question.

Let us begin by distinguishing between learning and instruction. As we have already stated, when we use the term learning we ordinarily mean a situation in which a change in behavior has been described or explained. By the term instruction, we mean situations in which behavioral change is accomplished according to specific criteria of efficiency. Of course, whenever instruction is successful, we have learning. The point is that the term learning is used when we are trying to understand behavior and the term instruction is used when we are trying to arrange conditions for effecting learning.

The distinction between learning and instruction is like the distinction between certain concepts in the natural sciences and engineering. The scientist typically explains phenomena by means of constructs, while the engineer must build bridges, satellites, and rockets. The engineer allows phenomena to happen in as natural a way as possible in order to study the conditions under which desired outcomes can be achieved. In many cases, the engineer attempts to simulate natural conditions (for example, in a wind tunnel) so that their effects on a particular phenomenon can be observed and described.

Because the scientist is concerned with phenomena under idealized conditions, his description does not apply directly to the natural state. Ultimately, the scientist argues that his description is more powerful in that he is able to account for a domain of phenomena while the engineer can account for only a limited number of events that he has observed in his laboratory. It is possible, of course, to have in practice not one or the other of these but some fruitful combination of the two.

Role of Educational Psychology

Educational psychology as an area of systematic concern within the domain of behavioral science has origins dating back to the publication of the *Journal of Educational Psychology* in 1910. Since that time, the field has reflected activities of both science and engineering. Although some have viewed educational psychology as purely an applied psychology, we argue that it is a field of inquiry with both theoretical and applied dimensions. That is, it is concerned with creating as well as verifying constructs.

A reasonable question for the practitioner to ask is why he should pay any attention to the activities of the psychologist. We would like to be able to say that knowledge or principles of behavior derived from the laboratory are essential to success in changing the behavior of others. After all, one should not be able to build satellites or rockets without some knowledge of the principles that describe the motion of bodies. However, it does not seem necessary that practitioners have a knowledge of scientific principles of behavior in order to be successful in shaping it.

There are a variety of ways in which we can know about behavior, and psychology is only one of these. Novelists and writers can tell us much about the motives and the conditions of behavior as can teachers, animal trainers, and parents. In fact, anyone who writes about or is forced to deal systematically with the behavior of others develops intuitive models for behavior as well as the nature of its major controlling variables.

Each of us has an intuitive model for behavioral phenomena. We are organisms ourselves and we develop frameworks or models that we use to predict the behavior of others. On the basis of an intuitive model we might predict, for example, that, if we walk into a roomful of strangers, extend our hand and announce our name, people will respond by extending their hands and announcing their names. At a more abstract level, most people would agree that the consequences of a specific behavior will surely affect the occurrence of that behavior in the future. Stated another way, it seems that the laws of conditioning and learning, which we shall presently discuss, are so obvious it is a wonder anyone had to discover them.

Once we understand how behavior is controlled, we may transmit such understandings to other individuals. By this process, we save others the task of having to discover these rules for themselves. Examples of this sort of activity are the animal trainer who helps us train our dog when we take him to obedience school and the master teacher who trains other teachers using principles that he has developed as a result of experience with children in a classroom. And, of course, we have parents who train their children using principles derived in one way or another from their own upbringing. Perhaps more often in today's anxious society, we use principles in this latter case that are formulated by individuals who are judged to be successful trainers of children. These principles are principles of practice, as are the principles used by the teacher and the animal trainer.

What can we expect the study of educational psychology to contribute to our knowledge of behavior? In one sense, knowledge of the scientific principles that underlie behavior can be used to predict performance when the trainer, teacher, or parent is faced with a new situation to which prescientific principles and practical intuitions do not apply. Since principles of practice are typically developed by trial and error, they account for only particular situations. To be sure, the same trial and error procedures can be used to discover appropriate principles in new situations. However, it is more efficient to use scientific principles of behavior to suggest new principles of training. These principles can be helpful in avoiding trial-and-error situations and in setting the boundaries within which new training procedures are developed.

In another sense, a knowledge of the scientific principles of behavior contributes to our understanding of the capabilities of the organisms with which we work. On purely esthetic grounds, one can argue that individuals who work with a phenomenon, behavioral or otherwise, should be aware of the principles that describe it.

In this book, we take the position that the science of psychology provides us with models that can be used in shaping behavior, that is, from which we can derive principles of instruction. Although we have our own preconceived models for behavioral change, these models lack generality, and it is generality that gives us the power to cope with a wide variety of situations. We are concerned with general principles of behavior as they have been derived from the laboratory setting and we shall also try to understand principles on the level of training and teaching (principles of practice) as they are generated from intuitive data gathered in the natural environment.

To restate an earlier point, models for behavior that have served as explanatory tools in the science of psychology enable us to understand behavior and the variables that affect it. Because we have our own preconceived models for the human organism as well as for lower animals, it is important to make them explicit and to relate them to the more powerful models of psychology; by so doing, we see our own behavior and the behavior of others as instances of a more general case.

Our goal is to understand specific facts, concepts, and principles in the science of psychology and the way in which they are related by means of models to behavior. It is the generality embodied in these models that we can use in practical situations when particular facts, concepts, and principles have deserted us or seem to be irrelevant. In other words, it is what we think the organism is that determines how we shall treat him when facts from the laboratory or our own experience cannot be applied.

A Framework for Understanding Behavior

To understand behavior, we must first describe it. A moment's reflection will reveal, however, that we are continually faced with a bewildering variety of behaviors, our own as well as others. And, if we are to understand these phenomena as well as the conditions under which they occur, we must break them down into manageable units.

We can begin to reduce the complexity of behavior by focusing our attention on something that interests us. Thus, we may ask about how children learn in a classroom, how a dog learns to sit up and beg, how our children learn to misbehave in certain ways to attract our attention, or how we learn to ride a bicycle or drive a car. We then break each of these problems or interests into units that we call behavioral systems.

The idea of a system is very general in science. In the study of behavior we describe the various states of particular behavioral systems and the conditions under which these states occur. In order to describe the states of a system and the way in which they change over time, we must be able to measure and count. The things that we measure and count are called variables. By convention, we define two classes of variables—independent and dependent.

In science, the major independent variable is time. For example, in the study of Newtonian mechanics, we describe the ways in which the states of a particular system such as a falling body change with time. In the case of behavior, time is also a major independent variable as, for example, when we wish to know how well an individual is doing on some task by observing his learning score (measure of behavior change) as a function of practice. Or we may wish to know how much has been forgotten as a function of the time since learning.

Although time is a major independent variable in almost every science, it is important to realize that it is only a reference variable. By this we simply mean that time in and of itself is not responsible for the change in the dependent variable that we observe. Rather, it is the events that occur in time that are responsible for such change. The goal of any science is to construct models for the processes that occur in time and that are responsible for changes in some dependent variable.

Obviously, in psychology the dependent variable is behavior. But behavior is a very general term (for example, whatever anyone does) and we speak of it in terms of components called performances or responses. As we progress through this book, we shall see that there are a variety of conventions for describing behavior.

In the study of learning, we are concerned with the conditions that determine changes in some measure of performance. By establishing relationships between independent and dependent variables through experimentation, we are able to describe the way a behavioral system changes with time. Once having mapped such changes, we propose mechanisms or models to account for them.

The Problem of Knowledge

One term we can use to label behavior is knowledge. However, "knowledge" is not often used by the experimental psychologist to describe the behavior of subjects in his laboratory. Yet, it is precisely terms such as knowledge, together with related terms such as meaning and understanding, that are at the heart of behavioral systems that comprise most complex learning situations. We say, for example, that students "know" the concept of culture or gene and that such "knowledge" is critical to the educational process.

We shall see that knowledge can be behavioralized by asking ourselves or others what an individual should be able to do who knows a concept such as culture. Often, however, such a procedure is not entirely satisfactory in that what we mean by knowledge is not some specific behavior or set of behaviors, but the way in which these behaviors are organized. More specifically, what we mean when we say that an individual knows a concept is that he can produce responses that are novel but appropriate in a wide variety of situations. Given a new situation, he can respond appropriately and, because the situation is new, we are assured that the response he has produced was not learned as such but was generated from some internal structure or organization.

We shall argue that it is the problem of describing knowledge that gives educational psychology its theoretical dimension. The problem of knowledge also serves as a meeting ground for theoretical and applied educational psychology. In the applied sense, the practitioner or behavioral engineer is concerned largely with putting behavior under precise external control. However, very often in a school situation we do not have any good idea of the events that control the behavior we want to change. Except for situations that we might characterize as obedience training, we cannot specify the knowledge that we wish to communicate.

Language

A major emphasis in our study of learning is language, particularly when we concern ourselves with teaching and the communication of knowledge. Not only is language a major vehicle for the storage and transmission of knowledge in our society but even in relatively simple situations, where we attempt to memorize or discriminate between objects, language can play an important role. This has led to speculation that our language provides us with the basic categories in terms of which we perceive experience. The Hopi Indians, for example, might see the world differently than we do because their language does not contain any term for the concept of time. And the Zuni Indian in South America may not discriminate among certain colors in the spectrum because their language provides them with no labels for these colors.

In our discussion of relatively simple learning situations, we shall find that the psychologist uses terms such as contiguity, frequency, and reinforcement to explain behavioral change. However, in more complex situations that embody language, such as those found in the home and school, it is sometimes necessary to define behavior so that it is not under the control of external forces. Nor does behavior necessarily obey laws of contiguity and frequency. This is due to the central role that language plays in many of the human being's specific characteristics. Human behavior is controlled largely by its own internal relations. And the individual transcends the effects of reinforcement, contiguity, and frequency through his ability to store and internalize his environment through language.

School Learning

"School learning" means that process in which the mechanisms of learning operate within the bounds set by the phenomenon of schooling to accomplish the goals of education. School learning is a process in which mechanisms of learning are engaged or brought into play by the environmental context of schooling. The major independent variable of school learning is the curriculum and the major dependent variable is achievement. In order to describe the ways in which these variables are related to one another we must come to grips with learning as it arises as a concept in experimental psychology, and as it is related to concepts of teaching and knowledge in educational psychology. But more than this, we must also attempt to understand how the term learning is involved in the problems encountered by individuals in everyday experience.

Suggested Readings

Ausubel, D. & Robinson, F. G. *School Learning*. Holt, Rinehart and Winston. 1969. An extensive book containing a wealth of information. Chapter 1 is a useful analysis of the nature and scope of educational psychology.

Belth, M. *Education as a Discipline*. Allyn and Bacon, Inc. 1965. A highly original work whose dense prose has probably prevented a wide reading. The first 60 pages should be read by anyone interested in the study of education.

Holt, J. *How Children Learn*. Pitman Publishing Co. 1967. An analysis of the learning process in children by one of the new generation of "angry young men." Many of Holt's points about the relevance of psychology for education are well taken and worth careful thought.

Jackson, P. W. *Life in Classrooms*. Holt, Rinehart and Winston. 1968. A modern account of the phenomenon of schooling by a distinguished educational psychologist and perceptive observer of children's behavior.

James, W. *Talks to Teachers*. W. W. Norton and Co. 1958. A classic. Although written over 60 years ago, many of the ideas are as relevant today as they were when James proposed them. It is an example of the intuitions of a brilliant psychologist about the psychology of school learning.

Rosenthal, R. & Jacobson, L. *Pygmalion in the Classroom.* Holt, Rinehart and Winston. 1968. A startling book on the notion of the self-fulfilling prophecy in education (that is, that children become what we think they are). The book has, however, been subjected to considerable methodological criticism.

Stephens, J. M. *Process of Schooling.* Holt, Rinehart and Winston. 1967. The phenomenon of schooling is described in considerable detail largely from an anthropological point of view. The book also contains a good summary and critique of methods research.

Walton, J. & Kuethe. *The Discipline of Education.* Univ. of Wisconsin Press. 1963. Much of this book is relevant to the ideas found in the preceding chapter. Of particular interest is the chapter by James Deese on the study of education by educational psychologists.

2
Describing Behavior

"When I use a word," Humpty Dumpty said, in rather
a scornful tone, "it means just what I choose it to mean—
neither more nor less."
"The question is," said Alice, "whether you can make
words mean so many different things."
"The question is," said Humpty Dumpty, "which is to
be master—that's all."

To understand behavioral change we must describe it. Although
description can be accomplished on a relatively informal level based
on our ideas about the relevant variables, these will often vary from
situation to situation. The psychologist attempts to describe all behavioral phenomena in the same way, thereby permitting a comparison
of different situations, with the ultimate possibility of linking them empirically as well as theoretically.

To describe behavior generally we need a common language
containing a set of terms with precise meanings. One such language
that is not unique to psychology, but is part of the scheme used by
any science to discuss phenomena, is derived from the idea of a system
discussed in Chapter 1.

Some Terminology

The first term we shall consider in this language is "function," by
which we mean simply a device for pairing numbers. A function is

10

a way of talking about the covariation of one thing with another. We state a function mathematically by an equation such as $y = f(x)$. By convention we call x in this equation the independent variable and y the dependent variable. This simply means that the values or numbers that are the y's are determined by the values or the numbers that are the x's.

An example of a functional relationship is that the amount of money (m) that one earns is a function of how many hours he works (Hw) if he is paid on an hourly basis $[m = f(Hw)]$. We might also say that the time (t) that it takes an object to reach the earth is a function of the height (h) from which it is dropped $[t = f(h)]$. Another example of a functional statement would be that the height (H) of an individual is a function, up to some point, of his age (A), $[H = f(A)]$. Notice that in each of these cases we have not specified the precise form of the functional relationship.

There are innumerable things in our environment that we could attempt to describe in terms of their covariation with other things; and although science is concerned with describing aspects of our environment that covary (the search for regularities), it is clear that we must be selective in what we attend to—a science cannot, after all, describe everything. This selectively is governed by the ideas that we have concerning what we are looking for (our theory).

Simple functional relationships are most easily represented in terms of graphs. A graph typically consists of a set of two orthogonal (perpendicular) axes along which we can plot values of the independent and dependent variables. Figure 2-1 represents the velocity (v) of a freely falling object as a function of time (t). It is worth pointing out that in the natural sciences we are more likely to find precise statements of functional relationships such as $v = gt$ (g being a constant) for the falling body. Since in the behavioral sciences we have few such precise statements, we must rely much more heavily on graphical displays of data.

By convention, the vertical axis in Figure 2-1 is labeled the ordinate and the horizontal axis is termed the abscissa. We plot values of the independent variable along the abscissa and values of the dependent variable along the ordinate.

We can use the concept of function or functional relationship to talk about behavioral change or learning. This is usually done by viewing behavioral change as a dependent variable and practice (time) as an independent variable. Figure 2-2 represents a typical finding when we plot a measure of performance as a function of practice. In this case,

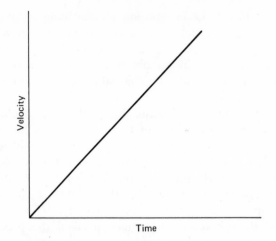

FIGURE 2-1

Velocity of a freely falling object as a function of time.

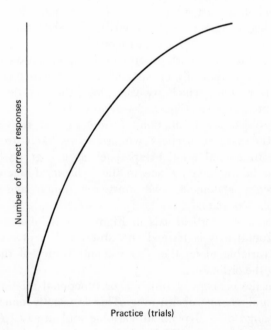

FIGURE 2-2

Number of correct responses as a function of practice.

the number of trials (time) that it takes an individual to learn is plotted on the abscissa and the change in his performance (how well he does) is plotted on the ordinate.

There are two ways in which we can talk about functional relationships such as those presented in Figures 2-1 and 2-2. We can begin with the statement of a functional relation in the form $y = f(x)$, arbitrarily assign values to the independent variable x, and then compute the values of the dependent variable y. We can then plot these points on the axes that define the graph, and connect them, thereby obtaining a line (curve). In science, however, we often work in the reverse direction. That is, we find values for the independent and dependent variables in the laboratory and plot these as points on a graph; we then attempt to write a functional relationship to mathematically describe the curve we have plotted. The value of constructing a functional relationship is that we can predict values of the dependent variables for new values of an independent variable.

When we write a functional relationship in the form $y = f(x)$, we assume continuous rather than discrete variables. In other words, we assume that we can draw a smooth curve through the points on the graph. In many cases, when the functional relationship is not known, we use straight lines between points on the graph to indicate that we do not know exactly what happens between the points.

Let us now rewrite the functional relationship in a form more appropriate for describing behavioral change. The dependent variable, y, is performance or the individual's response (R), and x, the independent variable, is an environmental event or stimulus (S). The functional relationship states that the response an individual makes in a given situation is in some way a function of a stimulus in that situation $[R = f(S)]$. We can, of course, elaborate this basic relationship and say that responses are a function not of a single environmental event but of many different stimuli and are also a function of the amount of time that we have been exposed to these stimuli. Thus, we might write our functional relationship $R = f(S_1, \ldots S_n, t)$. There are now $n + 1$ (n stimuli plus time) independent variables and one dependent variable described by the equation. The statement embodied in such a functional relationship is that the behavior of an individual is a function of events in his environment and time relationships between these events.

It is not necessarily implied in a functional relationship that the independent variables control the dependent variable, although in describing behavior we often see it this way. We say, for example, that the behavior of an individual is under the control of certain stimuli in his environment, and that if we manipulate those stimuli, his behavior will change accordingly. However, this is a special interpretation that is imposed on the basic functional description of behavior. It is important to realize that the functional relationship itself carries no such implications; it simply means that the two variables vary together in some systematic way.

To summarize, four terms have been introduced thus far. These are independent variable, dependent variable, function, and graph. These terms are at the heart of all experimentation done in any science. Experimentation is concerned with manipulating certain things that we call independent variables and seeing what difference they make in phenomenon that we index by a choice of dependent variables. In psychology, independent variables are portions of our environment and dependent variables are aspects of our behavior.

Some Criteria for Description

The defining characteristics of any experimental situation are its independent and dependent variables. Since it is possible that there may be a variety of relationships between events and responses, we design experiments to find the events that make the most difference in the behavior we are interested in studying. To do this, we assign values to the independent variables. We then present these values (stimuli) to the organism and observe whether there is any change in the dependent variable (behavior).

In order to successfully describe behavior in this way, we must make sure that only one thing is varying at a time. That is, if we want to attribute a change in behavior to the values we have assigned to an independent variable, we must make certain that no other independent variable is also changing its values at the same time.

This is one of the most important rules in describing any behavioral situation; namely, that we must hold everything in the situation constant except the variables whose effect on behavior we are studying. However, it is one thing to say that we want to hold constant all possible variables and quite another matter to determine the relevant extraneous variables. Let us consider a standard example of the role of extraneous variables in changing behavior. This example is often called the Placebo experiment.

We ask whether a particular drug (say, LSD) makes a difference in some behavior that we have chosen to observe (for example, talking—that is, the frequency of certain speech patterns). We administer the drug in pill form to an individual or sample of individuals and then observe their behavior. Of course, it is possible that it is not the drug in the pill but simply the act of taking the pill that has resulted in a change in behavior. We must therefore have a second individual or group of individuals who also receive pills, but harmless ones called placebos (that do not contain LSD). Since we have two groups, both of which take identical-looking pills but only one of which contains the drug under study, we can attribute any differences in behavior between the two groups to the drug.

We can only attribute differences in the behavior of individuals in the two groups to the drug if the two groups are identical in the beginning. If the two groups are not identical, it is possible that the differences are not due to any values of the independent variable, namely, the drug, but rather to properties of the individuals that comprise the groups (for example, more highly verbal individuals in one group than another).

Experimental control is another major concept that is part of any description of behavior. It is important to note that by experimental control we do not mean the absence of variables but that we have chosen another independent variable and assigned values to it. In the placebo experiment, we assigned the value "no content," so to speak, to the non-LSD pill. In many situations, however, several independent variables are manipulated at the same time and one variable may serve to control for another. The essential concept embodied in the idea of experimental control is that we want to make inferences about the influence of certain things on behavior, and we are only able to make these inferences provided that we know no other things could have made the difference that are found.

Inference is another concept used to describe behavior. We want to be able to say, for example, that when we find that a certain independent variable makes a difference in what a sample of subjects do, this variable will also make a similar difference in the behavior of a much larger group of individuals, often called a population, from which our sample of subjects was taken. If our sample of subjects in the experimental situation is representative of this larger group, we can make this inference or assertion.

Although it is standard practice to concern ourselves with sampling subjects in order to make inferences about the behavior of a larger group, we sometimes forget that it is also possible to sample independent and dependent variables. In other words, if the variable under consideration is some aspect of words, then we must sample words from the larger domain to which we wish to make inferences. When this domain is language itself, our words must be sampled from language. It is for this reason that research on nonsense syllables does not tell us very much about the behavior of individuals when they are using actual words. In like manner, it is important to sample tasks. Those things that we ask individuals to do in the laboratory must be representative of things that they do outside of the laboratory if we are to make any reasonable inferences about the dependent variables we have used (that is, whether the independent variables we have manipulated will affect what people ordinarily do).

Now that we have introduced some key concepts, we shall consider another example of the use of experimental control in making inferences about behavior. One standard situation in school learning involves the problem of assessing the effect on achievement of a new teaching method or curriculum. For this example, the independent variable is a new method of teaching geography. We shall call it method A. We want to know whether this new method is better than some previous method of teaching geography (method B). To answer this question we begin by describing the situation in which A and B are presented to pupils.

Let us suppose that we carefully choose two classrooms of individuals and that these individuals are assumed to be alike. That is, we have randomly assigned individuals into the two classrooms so that we can assume the two classrooms do not differ systematically in any way. We now use method A in one classroom and method B in the other (with the same teacher in each case). After some period of time, we give the pupils a test of achievement in geography and find that those individuals who have had teaching method A (the new method) do considerably better than those individuals who have had method B (the old method).

What can we conclude from this experiment? First, notice the similarity between this example and our previous one in which we used LSD. Perhaps in this case it is not the fact that teaching method A was better per se but that any method other than the standard method B would be better. In other words, given that A is used rather than the standard method, perhaps it is simply the fact that A is different from what students are used to and that they are getting some additional attention because the new method of teaching has been used (the so-called Hawthorne Effect).

The Hawthorne Effect says simply that the differences between two teaching methods is not due to the content of the methods but to the fact that an old method has been contrasted with a new one and that any new method would probably have the same effect in terms of student achievement. To control for the Hawthorne Effect, we would need groups of students who are taught by methods other than A or B so that A can be compared with these as well as with the standard method.

A Framework for Description

The term "design" is used to refer to the way in which we arrange independent variables in relation to the question we wish to ask. For example, we must arrange the independent variables so that we have the proper experimental controls and so that only one thing varies at a time. We also want to arrange the independent variables so that they are not confounded. That is, we want to make sure that as we change the value of one independent variable the value of another independent variable does not also change. We shall now consider several standard types of designs.

Two Randomized Groups

Our first task is to select an independent variable that varies in at least two respects so that we can assign it two values. These two values we call treatments, conditions, or methods. The question we want to ask is whether these two treatments differentially affect the value of the dependent variable.

To answer this question we must decide on a population of individuals whose behavior we wish to describe. We then sample a certain number of individuals at random from this population and randomly assign these individuals to the two groups in our experimental situation. Sampling randomly from the population simply means that we leave it to chance which individuals we use; random assignment means that we leave it to chance which individuals are put into which group. And, as a matter of fact, we assume that the average score of subjects on the dependent variable would be the same in the two groups at the start of the experiment. By chance, we could end up with two very different or unequal groups, but we assume that this does not happen. Later, we shall see that there is a procedure to insure that our two groups do not differ on the value of the dependent variable at the beginning of the experiment.

Once we have sampled our subjects randomly and assigned them randomly to two groups, the next step is to administer different values of the independent variable to the subjects in each group and to measure their behavior. It is important that the two groups be treated in exactly the same way except for the independent variable being manipulated and that we measure their behavior in precisely the same way. After the values of the independent variable have been administered and we have scored the behavior of subjects in the two groups, we compare the scores. If they are different and our situation has been constructed according to the rules just stated, we can attribute the difference between the two groups to the treatments or values of the independent variable, provided the difference is of a sufficient size.

In this book, we shall not be concerned with the issue of how large a difference in behavior must be in order to be a reliable or statistically significant finding. Suffice it to say that we want to make sure that the observed difference is large enough so that we cannot attribute it to chance differences between the two groups. It is worth noting that the difference we observe need not be large in order to be reliable. This means that, if we were to take successive samples of subjects from the same population, we would find the same difference in the same direction as before. The difference is reliable, but not large.

Two Matched Groups

It is possible that the difference in performance between our two groups of subjects could be due to the fact that they were different to begin with because even though we sample subjects randomly, by chance the two groups may not be equal. Therefore, we need a procedure for assuring that the groups are initially equal. Such a procedure is called a matched groups design. By matched groups we mean that we give our subjects a pretest before they are assigned to the experimental groups. Ideally, this pretest should be exactly the same test that we administer after the independent variable. However, because a pretest on the dependent variable might affect the results of the experiment, we often try to choose pretests that are related to the values of the dependent variable that we wish to measure. If, for example, we wish to observe the effect of some teaching method on achievement, we might try to match subjects in our two groups on IQ, since we suppose that IQ is a factor in achievement.

The essence of a matched groups design is that we sample subjects randomly from a population and then give them a pretest. Based on their scores on this test, we divide them into groups, for example, high, middle, and low IQ. We then take equal numbers of subjects from each of these three levels and assign them randomly to the two groups in the experimental situation, thus assuring ourselves that the same number of people with high-, middle-, and low-IQ scores is in each of the two experimental groups.

When we use a matching procedure, we must realize that there are a very large number of variables on which we could match subjects and that, in any experimental situation, we might choose unwisely. That is, we might not match individuals on variables that are relevant to the changes in behavior to be observed or we might match our two groups in such a way that the subsequent differences between them are due to our matching procedure itself rather than to the values of the independent variable.

The basic logic of the two groups design can be summarized as follows. We start with two groups that we are reasonably certain are equal. We then administer different values of an independent variable to each group. We note the changes in the dependent variable and make inferences from these changes to a larger population of subjects from which our individuals were chosen. In cases where our groups might be unequal by chance, we can use a matching procedure to assure ourselves that the groups are indeed equal.

Factorial Designs

In a factorial design, we have more than one value for each of two independent variables. As an example, consider two independent variables, such as the meaningfulness of passages of written material and amount of fatigue, where the dependent variable is reading speed. The passages we are comparing might be prose and nonsense material and the values of fatigue might be 12 hours without sleep versus 48 hours without sleep. We can diagram our choice of independent variables and the values of these variables as illustrated in Table 2-1 which also contains some hypothetical data.

From this table, we see that there are four possible combinations of variables and that we need four groups of subjects in order to administer one combination to each group. The major idea of factorial designs is embodied in the concept of interaction. Looking at the column means of Table 2-1, we might conclude that amount of fatigue is a determiner of reading speed. Looking at the row means in Figure 2-1 we might conclude that meaningfulness of material is a factor in reading speed. However, it might also be that reading speed is a function not of one variable or the other, but the way in which the two interact

TABLE 2-1

Average Number of Words Read Per Minute as
a Function of Meaningfulness and Fatigue

| | | Fatigue | | Row |
		12 hours	48 hours	Means
Meaningfulness	Nonsense	180	80	130
	Prose	280	280	280
	Column Means	230	180	

with one another. That is, fatigue may only make a difference in reading speed when we are asked to read nonsense material. When we read highly meaningful material, the amount of fatigue may not make a difference.

Let us try to illustrate the concept of factorial design by another choice of independent variables, perhaps one in which the idea of interaction is a little more apparent. Suppose that we want to ask which of two rifles is more accurate at 50 yards. Our dependent measure will be the number of hits within a certain diameter circle. In addition to asking which of the two rifles is better or more accurate, we also wish to ask which of two gunsights is better. We then have the design illustrated in Table 2-2. Notice that this design means that we attach each of the two gunsights to each of the two rifles. We have four combinations, one rifle with each of the two gunsights.

Looking at the column means in Table 2-2, we might conclude that rifle B is better than rifle A because the number of hits for B is greater than for A. On the other hand, if we look at the row means in Table 2-2 we might conclude that gunsight A is better than gunsight B for the same reason, that is, there were more hits in the bulls-eye with gunsight A than with gunsight B. Looking at just the row and column means, we might therefore predict that placing gunsight A on rifle B would be the optimal combination. But notice that, if we look in the body of the table at the number of hits in each of the four cells, we find that there were more hits with gunsight A and rifle A than with

TABLE 2-2

Number of Hits in a Bullseye as a Function
of Rifle and Gunsight

		Rifle		Row Means
		A	B	
Gunsight	A	13	9	11
	B	3	11	7
Column Means		8	10	

gunsight A and rifle B. The number of hits does not depend uniformly on which rifle or which gunsight is used, but rather on a particular combination of gunsight and rifle. This means that one gunsight works better with one rifle than with another, or it means that how good one of the gunsights is depends on which rifle we put it on.

Interaction means simply that the value of the dependent variable resulting from one independent variable is determined by the specific value assumed by the other independent variable. The idea of interaction can also be illustrated in our own preconceived model for behavior by the term "it depends." We might ask, for example, if it is more efficient, time-wise, for a man to put on his shirt or his trousers first while dressing in the morning. It could be that the answer is quite straightforward if, for all individuals we observe, putting on the shirt and then the trousers is the most efficient method. On the other hand, it might depend on how tall the man is. For tall men, it might be more efficient to put on the trousers first and then the shirt but, for short men, it might be more efficient to put on the shirt first and then the trousers. The statement "it depends" contains the basic idea of interaction.

Interactions can also be illustrated in graphs such as Figure 2-3. Here we find that the lines that describe the two types of rifles and the two types of gunsights actually cross. This graph clearly shows the interaction between rifle and gunsight; namely, that the number of hits

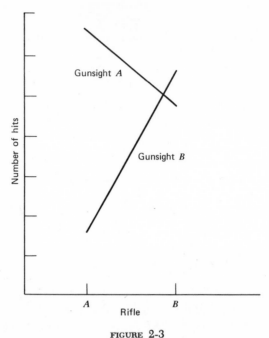

FIGURE 2-3

Interaction between types of rifle and gunsight.

with gunsight A and rifle A is greater than with gunsight B and rifle A, and that the number of hits with gunsight A and rifle B is less than with gunsight B and rifle B.

It is important to plot data in graphical form because the kinds of interactions that take place between independent variables are not always of the obvious sort that we just considered. As is illustrated in Figure 2-4, it might be the case that gunsight A is better with rifle A than gunsight B is with rifle A, but that gunsight A is even better with rifle B than gunsight B is with rifle B. In other words, the difference between the gunsights is greater with rifle B than with rifle A although in either case gunsight A is better than gunsight B. Although the lines in Figure 2-4 do not cross one another as they did in Figure 2-3, there is still an interaction. In answer to the question, "What is the effect of gunsight or rifle," we must say, "It depends."

Extraneous Variables

Extraneous variables in a given situation are things that could affect the value of our dependent variable and that are not manipulated in

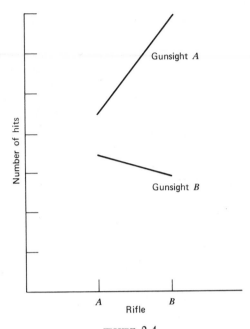

FIGURE 2-4

Interaction between types of rifle and gunsight.

the experimental design (that is, they are not independent variables). For example, consider our earlier situation in which we measured the effect of fatigue and meaningfulness of material on reading speed. Fatigue and meaningfulness are two independent variables that can be varied separately in a factorial design. At the same time, however, it is possible that the time of day in which we choose to run our experiment, the level of lighting in the room, the temperature of the room or any number of other variables might also affect reading speed. These other variables, which we do not manipulate directly, are called extraneous variables. Given the fact that we do not want to ask what their effect is on reading speed, we must be certain to control for them in our experimental situation.

We typically control for the effect of extraneous variables by testing all subjects at the same time under the same conditions so that any effect that these variables have on our dependent measure is equal for all subjects. Moreover, if we do this, it is not necessary to specify all possible extraneous variables. We must only be certain that all extraneous variables are present to an equal extent for all values of the independent variable under study.

It is worth noting that there is another way that we can control extraneous variables although the procedure is more often used in the natural rather than the social sciences. The procedure is to eliminate them altogether. For example, in the case of a body falling from a given height above the surface of the earth, some extraneous variables might be air resistance, temperature, and wind velocity. We remove the effects of such variables by conducting our experiment in a vacuum or in a situation that approximates a vacuum as nearly as possible. In this way, we eliminate all variables except the one of interest, namely, the height above the earth. We could accomplish the same thing for behavior by conducting experiments in rooms that are designed to eliminate as many distracting variables as possible, for example, rooms that have been soundproofed to eliminate the effects of unwanted noise. However, in the behavioral sciences, extraneous variables are most often taken into account by equating the conditions under which the experiment is conducted rather than by precise experimental control.

Confounding

Another concept that we must discuss in order to understand how behavioral situations can be described is "confounding." By confounding we mean that two or more independent variables vary together in a perfectly correlated fashion in a given experimental situation. Because these two independent variables are perfectly correlated, it is not possible to attribute any differences in behavior to one or the other.

Let us consider an example. Figure 2-5 illustrates an experiment in

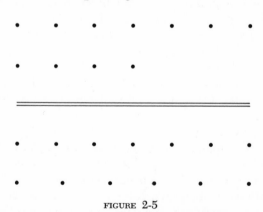

FIGURE 2-5

Top: Number of dots confounded with length of array.
Bottom: Number of dots independent of length of array.

which we ask about the independent variables that affect a child's judgment of the number of dots appearing in a linear array. Notice that, in the first portion of Figure 2-5, the length of the array of dots and the number of dots in the array is completely confounded. That is, long arrays of dots contain a large number of dots and short arrays of dots contain few dots. Thus, when the child chooses a long array as containing more dots than a short array, we cannot be certain that he has made his choice because there are more dots in the long array or simply because the array is longer (that is, he has responded to length rather than to number). What we need in order to break the confounding in the situation is a short array that contains the same number of dots as a long array or two arrays of the same length and a different number of dots. In this fashion, we separate the independent variable of length of the array from the independent variable of the number of dots.

Another source of confounding arises when we use the same subjects rather than different groups of subjects for each value of the independent variable. If we adopt the strategy of giving a single group of subjects more than one value of the independent variable, we must consider order effects; namely, the order in which the independent variables are presented is a relevant variable in determining the performance of subjects. Suppose that we give students an arithmetic test, an algebra test, and then a physics test in that order. We can be reasonably certain that subjects who received the physics test after having previously taken both an arithmetic test and an algebra test are not the same individuals and will not perform in the same way as subjects who received the physics test without the two prior mathematics tests. If we want to ask about the effect of having the physics test last, we must choose at least one other group of subjects. This group would receive the physics test without the arithmetic and algebra tests first. We could also ask whether the order of the two mathematics tests makes a difference in physics test performance, in which case we would choose still another group and give them the algebra test first, then the arithmetic test, and then the physics test.

In describing any behavioral situation, it is important to ask ourselves what the possible independent variables are that can affect the behavior we are interested in observing. We must then be certain that these independent variables are varied separately so that we can attribute changes in behavior to them individually or in combination with one another as in a factorial design.

Notice that the idea of confounding is different from interaction. In the case of confounding, we have two (or more) independent variables that affect behavior, but the situation has not been designed so that we can determine how these effects can be attributed to the two variables. In the case of interaction, we have controlled the independent variables separately and we can determine how behavior is affected by different values of the two independent variables or whether the behavior we observe is a function of a particular combination of the two variables operating together.

Individual Subject Design

Another frequently used design is the individual subject design in which we use a single subject and examine his behavior extensively over a period of time. The strategy here is to allow the subject to perform on a relevant task before the independent variable has been administered so that we can establish a base line of behavior. For example, if we are describing the behavior of a rat in a box who is learning to press a bar for food, we might want to know how often he presses the bar while randomly exploring the box—even when pressing the bar does not result in food. We then use this base line to assess the effect of a treatment such as varying the amount of food he receives for bar pressing. Individual subject designs are useful to the extent that we can very precisely control the environment and the extraneous variables that can influence the organism's performance. As in the case of the natural sciences, if we could eliminate all possible extraneous variables, individual subject designs would be optimally efficient. However, since it is difficult to place human beings under such precise experimental control, we typically use designs involving more than one subject.

Additional Designs

Let us now consider a final example, one which concerned early educational psychologists such as Edward L. Thorndike. The situation is as follows: We present subjects with material, in this case Latin, and ask them to learn it. We then give them a second subject matter, German, and ask whether they will learn German better now than if they had not previously learned Latin.

In order to ask this question, we need at least one other group of subjects; namely subjects who have not had the opportunity to learn Latin before learning German. In Table 2-3 we see a two-group design in which the independent variables are Latin and not-Latin. This is

TABLE 2-3

Basic Transfer Design to Investigate Effects of Learning
Latin on Learning German

	Learn	Learn	Test
Group 1	Latin	German	German
Group 2	. . . . .	German	German

the simplest form of what we shall later call a transfer design. We can equate subjects ahead of time on variables such as IQ, sex, and achievement or we can randomize subjects and assign them to the two groups without concern for matching variables. We say that the group that received no pretraining in Latin is a control group and the group that received Latin first and then German is the experimental group. By comparing the performance of the two groups on a test of German, we attribute the differences between them to having learned Latin.

Someone might ask, however, whether learning Latin contributed to better performance on German or whether any foreign language would have sufficed. Might not, for example, learning French have the same effect on learning German as learning Latin had? We can enhance our design by adding a third group of subjects who learn French first and then German. The argument could be further extended to another language, such as Spanish. The idea is that, rather than something peculiar to Latin, that which contributes to better performance on German is the fact that the individual has had to learn two languages. By adding additional groups of subjects, we are able to pin down the effects of the independent variable and thus be more precise about our description of behavior.

We might also try to be more analytical by asking what there is about Latin or any other foreign language, for that matter, that contributes to the observed effects on learning German. To do this, we might try to break Latin up into a variety of components (grammar, vocabulary, and so forth) and make each of these components an independent variable in its own right. We could then administer Latin grammar or Latin vocabulary to groups of subjects and have them perform on tests of German after the appropriate course work in the German language. The attempt to partition a given task into a variety of components is at the heart of modern work using transfer designs to study the nature of learning.

Summary

In behavioral situations, the dependent variable that is always of interest is the individual's performance or response (R). We ask whether R is a function of some stimulus condition or treatment that has been administered to the organism. We might also ask whether responses are a function of some state of the organism (O). In this case, our functional relationship takes the form $R = F(O)$ rather than $R = F(S)$. Of course, it is possible that the responses the subject makes are not a function of prior stimuli or some internal state, but of previous responses. So we also have the condition where R is a function of R, $[R = F(R)]$. This is described as a correlational rather than experimental or cause and effect relationship. For example, we might predict performance on a physics test from performance on an algebra test.

The functional relationships that we shall be considering throughout the remainder of this book are of the form $R = F(S_1, \ldots S_n)$ where R is the behavior we observe and where the S's refer to stimulus conditions. We can generalize this functional relationship to the form $R = F(S_1, \ldots S_n, M, t)$ where M stands for the motivational state of the organism and t stands for time or practice. The responses that an individual makes are a function of many things, and it is our job to specify as many of these variables as possible. The important thing to realize is that each thing that we suspect affects behavior is a candidate for an independent variable. By treating conditions that affect behavior as independent variables, we are able to attribute performance to them in precise and well-defined ways. Without such a description, our understanding of behavioral situations remains at an intuitive level from which it is very difficult to make accurate predictions.

Suggested Readings

Bachrach, A. J. *Psychological Research.* Random House. 1966. A paperback that provides a good overview of some of the problems and rewards of the laboratory study of behavior. Chapter 5 on the laboratory and the "real world" is particularly worthwhile.

Hyman, Ray. *The Nature of Psychological Inquiry.* Prentice-Hall, Inc. 1964. A perspective on the "scientific method" in behavioral research. Chapter 4 is a stimulating critique on the "mystical world" of scientific facts.

Kerlinger, F. *Foundations of Behavioral Research*. Holt, Rinehart and Winston. 1964. A compendium of research methods. To be kept within reach when attempting one's first foray into the laboratory. Chapter 1 on the nature of science is a useful complement to our point of view.

McGuigan, F. J. *Experimental Psychology*. Prentice-Hall, Inc. 1960. Complete emphasis on methodology. Not to be confused with what is ordinarily referred to as experimental psychology. Chapters 5–10 are a good introduction to the design of experiments.

Sax, G. *Empirical Foundations of Educational Research*. Prentice-Hall, Inc. 1968. A "how to do it" manual for the uninitiated. Chapters 1 and 2 contain useful discussions of the relationship between science and educational research.

Underwood, B. J. *Psychological Research*. Appleton-Century-Crofts. 1957. The thoughts of one of our best present day experimental psychologists on the tactics and strategies of scientific research. Chapters 1–5, which emphasize research designs and operational definitions, are excellent.

Underwood, B. J. *Experimental Psychology*. Appleton-Century-Crofts. 1968. A fairly standard treatment of classical experimental psychology. Chapter 4 on experimental design is good additional reading on randomized and matched groups research designs.

3
Models of
Learning

"Can you do Addition?" the White Queen asked.
"What's one and one and one and one and one and one and
one and one and one and one?"
"I don't know," said Alice. "I lost count."
"She can't do Addition," the Red Queen interrupted.
"Can you do Subtraction? Take nine from eight."
"Nine from eight. I can't, you know," Alice replied very
readily; "but—"
"She can't do Subtraction," said the White Queen.
"Can you do Division? Divide a loaf by a knife—what's the
answer to that?"

Our task in this chapter is twofold. First, we shall describe briefly
the way in which we look at changes in behavior in order to determine
whether or not learning has occurred. Second, we shall describe some
models that are used to account for specific kinds of learned behavior.

One way to determine whether learning has taken place is to construct
a graph such as the one in Figure 3-1. The dependent variable or
measure of performance is represented on the ordinate (vertical axis) and
the independent variable of time is represented on the abscissa (horizontal axis). When we examine performance changes as a function of time,
we ordinarily divide the abscissa into categories that we label intervals of
practice or trials. Our description of learning is then in terms of a relationship between changes in a measure of performance and increments
of practice.

The major dependent variables used to study performance changes

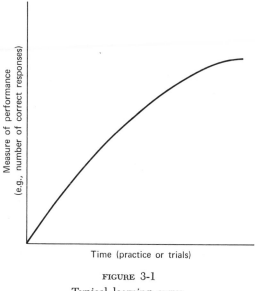

FIGURE 3-1
Typical learning curve.

are frequency or the number of responses, latency or speed of responding, and amplitude. These dependent variables can all be quantified using
standard measuring procedures. The major independent variables ordinarily used to study learning are frequency, contiguity and
reinforcement.

By frequency as an independent variable we mean how often an individual has been exposed to the situation in which he must learn to
behave appropriately. By contiguity we mean how close together in
either time or space events in the situation are to one another. And
by reinforcement we mean a condition under which the frequency of
some response increases as a result of stimuli that are either applied
to or withdrawn from the organism.

We can construct a learning or performance curve such as the one
in Figure 3-1 for each individual in a particular task. If we do so, we
find that the curves are quite erratic and seldom like the one in Figure
3-1. In describing a typical learning situation, we usually average performance scores across many subjects to obtain a group learning curve.
Such curves are generally smooth in character and increase as a function
of practices up to some maximum level. Notice that, instead of plotting
the number of correct responses, we could also plot errors as a dependent
variable (depending of course on the task). In this case, the learning

curve would decrease rather than increase over time since, in general, subjects become more accurate in their performance as a result of practice.

People often differ in the speed with which they learn. For example, some subjects may learn a list of words completely in five trials. Other subjects may take six trials and still others may take ten trials. If we plot our data as indicated in Figure 3-1, we fail to take account of the fact that subjects are reaching criterion performance (for example, two successive times through the list without errors) at different times during practice. A more adequate account of the learning that has taken place for a group of subjects is obtained in this case by dividing each subject's total learning time into an equal number of segments. In the case of a subject who learned the list in five trials, we divide his total learning time into five equal segments. The subject who took ten trials to learn the same material to the same criterion also has his learning time divided into five segments. On the horizontal axis or abscissa we then plot the average performance for each subject in each of the five intervals.

Since learning is a construct inferred from performance, we must be mindful of the fact that variables that affect performance may not necessarily indicate true learning. In order to separate behavioral changes that are permanent from those that are of a more transitory nature, we typically examine performance at two separate periods of time. An illustration of the nature of this description appears in Figure 3-2.

The independent variable of interest in Figure 3-2 is amount of reinforcement (for example, number of food pellets). We may ask whether amount of reinforcement differentially influences performance on some task such as lever pressing or running speed in the white rat. The learning curves in Figure 3-2 indicate that, for two groups of rats, during the first time interval high amounts of reinforcement result in better performance than low amounts of reinforcement. At Time 2 (for example, after 15 minutes of practice), we divide each of the two groups of subjects into two subgroups. Two of these subgroups continue with the same level or amount of reinforcement as before and two are changed to the other condition. If the behavior of the changed group in each case rapidly becomes like that of the group that continued on at the standard level of reinforcement, we say that there has been no permanent change in behavior and that amount of reinforcement is not a learning variable. But if performance of the changed groups (as illustrated by the dotted lines in Figure 3-2) differs from performance of

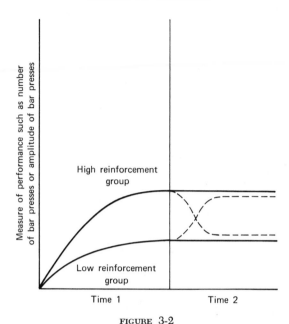

FIGURE 3-2

Performance as a function of amount of reinforcement.

the groups that remain at the standard conditions, we infer that something happened to the subjects during Time 1 that permanently affected
their behavior. Since the only thing that made the two groups different
at Time 1 was amount of reinforcement, we say that amount of reinforcement is a variable that affects learning.

The difference between performance that reflects learning and that
which does not can also be illustrated in a table such as Table 3-1.
The left hand margin in this table indicates values of the independent
variable (amount of reinforcement) at Time 1 and the horizontal or top
portion of the table reflects values of the independent variable at Time
2. The actual cell entries are scores of the subgroups at Time 2.

Column differences in Table 3-1 indicate differences in performance
as a function of different values of the independent variable at Time
2. Row differences in the table indicate performance differences at Time
2 as a function of values of the independent variable at Time 1. According to the data in Table 3-1 amount of reinforcement is a performance
variable but not a learning variable. In other words, it is possible to
find differences in performance at Time 2 that do not necessarily indicate
that learning has taken place. What this means is that when we remove

TABLE 3-1

A Sample Design to Determine the Effect of Amount of
Reinforcement on Learning and Performance

Time 2

	Low Reinforcement	High Reinforcement	Row Means
Time 1 — Low Reinforcement	4	16	10
Time 1 — High Reinforcement	6	14	10
Column Means	5	15	

the independent variable (in this case amount of reinforcement), behavior will fall to some base line level, whereas if true learning had
taken place, the behavior would no longer be the same as it was before
the independent variable was presented.

Type 1 Learning

Let up apply the above description of learning to some relatively simple
situations. The first situation we choose consists of two stimulus events
and two responses. For convenience, we shall call one of the stimulus
events the unconditioned stimulus (UCS). This stimulus reliably
elicits some response (for example, food leads to salivation). The response elicited by the unconditioned stimulus (that is, salivation) is
called the unconditioned response (UCR).

The second stimulus event is referred to as a conditioned stimulus
(CS). It does not elicit the unconditioned response elicited by the UCS,
although it may itself elicit unconditioned responses of other sorts (for
example, a bell may elicit pricking up the ears or head turning in an

animal but not salivation). If we present a CS and then a UCS many times in succession, we usually find that the CS will elicit a response like the UCR, which we call the conditioned response (CR). In other words, the bell will elicit salivation. We say that learning has occurred due to repeated pairings of the two stimulus events when the perviously neutral CS elicits the UCR or some portion of this response.

If the CR and UCR happen to occur together at the same point in time, it is not possible to decide whether learning has taken place. One way to see whether an association has been formed between the CS and CR is to observe whether the CR has moved ahead in time so that it occurs before the UCR (for example, if salivation occurs before the food is presented). Another way to test for learning in this situation is to remove the UCS altogether and see whether the CR will occur in its absence. The terms often used to refer to the situation we have just described are Pavlovian, classical, or respondent conditioning, and the most famous instance of this kind of learning is the dog that learned to salivate to the sound of a bell.

Once an association has been established between a CS and a CR, we can ask about the influence of independent variables on the strength of this association. For example, if we manipulate frequency of practice, we find that the more times the bell (CS) is followed by the food (UCS) the greater the amount of salivation (CR) we observe before the food is presented. The strength of association or relationship between the CR and CS then depends in a regular way on the number of times the two events (CS, UCS) have occurred.

We can also manipulate the temporal relationship between the CS and UCS as in independent variable. This is the variable we previously referred to as contiguity. The typical finding in this case is that in order for maximum learning to occur, the CS must precede the UCS by about one-half second.

If we continue to manipulate aspects of this situation, we discover that salivation will be elicited not only by the bell but also by a whole class of stimuli such as tones and loud noises which are similar to the initial CS. In other words, the organism has learned to make a conditioned response not only to the initial stimulus presented during learning but to the other simuli that are related in some way to the initial stimulus. We call this phenomenon stimulus generalization. It is a natural outcome of most learning situations.

Stimulus generalization means that stimuli other than the initial conditioned stimulus will elicit the conditioned response, though usually not as readily or as strongly. If we want to reduce this generalization so that the organism makes his response only to one particular stimulus, we must teach him not to respond under alternative conditions. One way to accomplish this is to withhold the UCS whenever a response is made to a stimulus other than the one we have chosen as correct. In the case of the dog salivating to the sound of the bell, we might withhold food if he salivates to any loud noises or to tones. We call this reduction of stimulus generalization discrimination learning.

If we choose to withhold the UCS altogether instead of just withholding it for those stimuli that are not judged to be appropriate, we find that the CR disappears from the organism's behavior. That is, the dog will no longer salivate to the sound of a bell if we cease to follow his salivation with presentation of food. This process of withholding the UCS and the subsequent deterioration of the CR is referred to as experimental extinction. If, at some later point in time, we again present the CS, we usually find that the CR reappears, although not as strongly as before. The reappearance of the CR following experimental extinction is called spontaneous recovery.

Once a stimulus has come to function as a CS in a learning situation, it can also play the role of a UCS for subsequent learning. In the Pavlovian situation, when the bell reliably elicits the response of salivation, it may be paired with another stimulus, such as a light, and after a sufficient number of pairings in which the light precedes the bell, the light may also lead to the response of salivation (that is, the light has become a CS).

The kinds of responses readily associated with stimuli, using the above procedures, are typically reflexes. We often refer to these reflex behaviors as respondents and thus we can term our conditioning procedure respondent conditioning. By contrast, we shall now consider the formation of associations that involve behaviors that are not reflexes and that, moreover, do not seem to be initially associated with any particular stimulus.

Type 2 Learning

To increase the frequency of "voluntary" behavior, we typically follow the occurrence of this behavior by a reinforcing stimulus. If, as a result of this procedure, the behavior occurs more often than it did before, we say that another kind of learning has occurred. This type of learning we call Skinnerian, instrumental, or operant conditioning and the behavior whose frequency of occurrence we have increased we call operant behavior.

We can characterize this situation as one in which we observe an organism and wait until he emits some kind of behavior whose frequency of occurrence we wish to increase. On the emission of this behavior, we present a stimulus that increases the frequency of the response. This stimulus is termed a reinforcing stimulus or simply a reinforcer.

The goal of this type of conditioning is to estabilsh a behavior in an organism that it did not previously make with any great frequency. A critical aspect of our procedure is that we present the stimulus only if the organism makes the desired response. Notice that this operation differs from the one employed in classical conditioning where we presented the UCS regardless of whether the conditioned response occurred. Since, in operant conditioning, we often do not know the stimulus that elicits the response of interest, we simply say that the response is emitted rather than elicited.

In effect, we have said to the organism that we have something he wants, namely, a reinforcer such as food, or praise or money and, in order for him to obtain it, he will have to do what we wish. A critical aspect of the situation is, of course, the organism's desire for the stimulus on which we make his behavior contingent.

As a working definition for our use of the term reinforcement, we adopt the convention illustrated in Table 3-2. Here, positive and negative stimuli are defined as anything that the organism will naturally seek out (for example, food, candy, toys, and money) or avoid (for example, shock, a spanking, "No," and "bad"). The rows in the table refer to either presenting or withdrawing such stimuli and the arrows within

TABLE 3-2

A Definition of Reinforcement

	Positive Stimulus	Negative Stimulus
Present	↑	↓
Withdraw	↓	↑

the cells indicate whether the frequency of behavior has been increased
(↑) or decreased (↓). By reinforcement, therefore, we mean any stimulus that increases the probability of some immediately preceding response. Positive and negative reinforcers are those events represented
by the two diagonal cells in which the arrows point upward. The other
two diagonal cells in Table 3-2 refer to conditions often associated with
the use of the term "punishment."

To determine additional properties of the operant conditioning situation, we once again manipulate independent variables and observe the
resulting changes in behavior. In typical experiments of this sort, the
first thing we notice is that the number of opportunities we allow for
the response and consequent reinforcing stimulus to occur together is
an important determiner of the speed with which the response will
occur. Recall that, in type 1 learning, the term "frequency" referred
to the pairing of the conditioned and unconditioned stimulus, while
in the second case, it refers to the pairing of a response and the reinforcing stimulus which follows it. A learning trial in the second
situation is never complete until the organism makes the desired
response. In the first situation, a learning trial is completed when the
unconditioned stimulus is presented and it is presented regardless of
whether the organism makes the conditioned response.

We may also manipulate contiguity as an independent variable. It
makes a good deal of difference whether the reinforcing stimulus follows
immediately on the emission of the behavior. If there is a considerable
delay in time between the response and the occurrence of the stimulus
that reinforces it, some other responses might appear and be
strengthened instead. This leads to what is sometimes referred to as
"superstitious behavior" on the part of the organism. This simply means
that what the organism has decided he must do in order to get reinforced
is different from what the experimenter is using as the basis for administering reinforcement.

The classical example of operant conditioning is the white rat that
learns to press a bar in a box for the reinforcement of food. Initially,
on being placed in the box, a naive rat will not press the bar for
food; but he will explore his environment since he has been deprived of
food for many hours, often until his body weight is only 80% of what it
normally would be. Eventually, in the course of exploring his environment, he will bump or in some fashion manipulate the bar that controls
the dispensing of food pellets. Once he has made this response, his behavior changes dramatically. In a short time, the rat presses the bar in a
fairly regular fashion and we say that learning has occurred.

If we study such an organism's behavior carefully, we can also observe that there is variability in his responses. We find, for example, that a rat will press the bar with his foot, with his elbow, and in some cases he may lean on it or back into it or perhaps even press it with his nose. This tendency for the conditioned response to appear in a variety of forms is referred to as response generalization. We can teach the rat to discriminate among these various responses by withholding the reinforcing stimulus for all responses but the desired one.

We can also teach the rat to discriminate among different stimulus situations by presenting the reinforcing stimulus only under certain conditions. For example, we might choose to reinforce the rat only when a tone appears. In this case, the rat is not reinforced if he makes a response when the tone is off. The rat learns to discriminate the presence and absence of the tone and will eventually make his response only under appropriate conditions. Once this discrimination has been established, we ordinarily find stimulus generalization just as we did in classical conditioning. In other words, the rat may respond by pressing the bar to a variety of tones. It is important to note that, in this case, stimulus generalization follows discrimination learning rather than precedes it. Given that we have stimulus generalization (for example, bar pressing to more than one tone), we can use selective reinforcement to teach the rat to respond to one particular tone as we did with the dog in Type 1 learning.

Discrimination training in the operant conditioning situation can be used to determine whether a nonverbal organism can make certain discriminations. We might want to know, for instance, whether a pigeon can see colors. To ask this question, we first train the pigeon to peck a key. Next, we introduce a discriminative cue—sometimes called an S^D. When a red light is on we reinforce his pecking response and when it is off we do not reinforce the response (the absence of the red light is referred to as an S^Δ condition). Eventually, the pigeon will peck the key only when the light is on. Now we begin to vary the color (hue) of the light, keeping things such as brightness as constant as possible. At first, because of stimulus generalization, the pigeon will peck to other colors. When he pecks to something other than red, however, we withhold reinforcement. If the pigeon can detect the change in color from one stimulus to the next, he will cease to respond to colors other than red. If he cannot detect differences in color, his pecking behavior will break down (become erratic) and may either stabilize at a reduced level or cease altogether, depending on the way we present the stimuli. The point is that, by using discrimination training procedures, we can "ask" a nonverbal organism certain kinds of questions. These procedures have also been used to teach pigeons to respond with the appropriate behavior to simple words such as "peck and "turn around."

Terminology

Our description of behavioral change in terms of classical and operant conditioning has been in terms of rather idealized performance situations. Moreover, we have not attempted to account for observed regularities in behavior in terms of internal states or processes. This latter kind of activity, constructing models for internal states or processes, amounts to building theories about the way in which events in the real world are related to behavior through mechanisms inside the organism.

When we construct models to account for observed regularities in behavior, we may or may not use the same language we used to describe performance in the first place. The language of stimuli and responses is probably the most popular performance language and, if we draw on this language for an explanation of performance regularities, we generate an explanatory model that consists of internal stimuli and internal responses. It is not necessary, however, to talk about learning in the same language that we use to talk about performance. We might talk about performance in terms of stimuli and responses and we might talk about learning in terms of scanning mechanisms and memory registers. There are difficulties, however, in using different language systems in discussing performance and learning.

The language used in this chapter to describe learning and performance allows us to state a number of conclusions about classical and operant conditioning. In one situation, we form a new association between existing reflex behaviors and selected stimulus conditions. In the other situation we watch for behavior to appear and then increase its frequency of occurrence by administering stimuli called reinforcers.

Our description of learning is in terms of relations between stimuli and responses that we have called associations. But what about the responses themselves? Where do new responses come from? How, for example, do children learn to talk? Are such responses built in and therefore strengthened or are they somehow learned and, if learned, with what are they associated? Moreover, how can we wait for responses to appear if they are not available in the first place? The classical conditioning model does not describe learning of any new responses, only the formation of new associations and their subsequent strengthening. Operant conditioning situations, on the other hand, can be used to describe how new (very infrequent) behaviors appear in the repertoire of the organism.

The major concept that we employ in describing how new responses are constructed is "shaping." By this term we mean simply that we look for some approximation to the response the frequency of which we wish to increase and, by reinforcing this behavior, we build a closer approximation to the chosen response. For example, consider a pigeon who is trained to peck a key. Initially, when we place the pigeon in a box containing the key, we reinforce him (give him food) simply for standing on the side of the box containing the key. The next step is to reinforce him whenever he turns in the direction of the key. We then reinforce him for bending his head down toward the key, then for bumping it, and, finally, for pecking it. Reinforcing approximations to a desired behavior is an extremely powerful tool for changing behavior.

At this point, it is worth reminding ourselves that the terminology we have used in talking about operant and classical conditioning situations represents observed behavior. Therefore, concepts such as generalization, discrimination, extinction, and spontaneous recovery can be used interchangeably in the two situations to the extent that the behaviors in question are equivalent. However, some terms, such as reinforcement and shaping, are more applicable to one situation than another.

It is also important to keep in mind that the two situations present somewhat different pictures of behavior. Classical conditioning presents a picture of learning in which an arbitrary stimulus is associated with a highly specific, elicitable response. The operant conditioning situation, on the other hand, describes the differentiation and discrimination of a response out of a mass of behavior emitted in response to a complex (undefined) stimulus field. The first situation stresses time control. The second stresses the role of motivation and reward.

Summary

As stated in the introduction, much of what we have to say about learning, as viewed through the classical and operant conditioning situations, is perhaps obvious. That is, the facts that we have stated are generally consistent with our own preconceived models of what behavior is and how it is affected. We might say that, except for gaining a consistent language to use in talking about behavioral phenomena and a specific model for interpreting relations in these phenomena, we have learned very little. In one sense, this is true. Certainly, an accomplished animal trainer sometimes employs principles consistent with what we have called operant conditioning, without ever being aware of our models or our language system. In like manner, when the classroom teacher attempts to teach the meaning of words in a foreign language, she may employ a conditioning situation. And, in parent-child relations, we find many examples of stimulus events, such as darkness and loud noise or harsh punishment, which are paired with generalized responses such as fear or anxiety.

Finding examples from everyday life that seem to fit the two kinds of learning situations described above is quite easy and, indeed, it should be. Because the behavior being described is obvious does not mean, however, that we cannot profit from a precise description of it. After all, the basic phenomena of motion were well known before Newton described them in precise terms. What is gained by scientific description is the potential for explanation, which means simply the possibility of fitting particular phenomena into a larger context thereby accounting for other phenomena as well. Out of this kind of activity eventually comes a theory for interpreting and dealing more efficiently with our environment.

Suggested Readings

Deese, J. & Hulse, S. *Psychology of Learning*. McGraw-Hill. 1967. A basic introductory text. The first half, which is devoted largely to animal learning, is a more thorough statement of many of the ideas contained in this chapter.

Gagne, R. M. (Ed.) *Learning and Individual Differences*. Charles E. Merrill Books, Inc. 1967. A book of contributed papers. The concluding chapter by Arthur Melton is a nice complement to his chapter in *Categories of Human Learning*.

Hilgard, E. & Bower, G. Theories of Learning. Appleton Century-Crofts. 1966. As originally authored by Hilgard, the book was a classic. Recently revised by Hilgard and Bower, the book continues to be influential although the general issue of learning theories is not as important as it once was. The introductory chapter on the nature of learning theories is extremely useful for anyone wishing to think critically about descriptions of learning behavior.

Keller, F. S. *Learning: Reinforcement Theory*. Random House. 1954. An older statement of the principles of operant conditioning. This is a short book, clearly and simply written. It repays thoughtful reading.

Kimble, G. *Conditioning and Learning*. Appleton-Century-Crofts. 1961. An advanced text to be read after such things as Deese and Hulse, and Smith and Moore. The discussion of learning in Chapters 1 and 2 can be read without extensive background, however, and should be read by those who want a thorough grasp of the issues involved in the study of learning.

McGeoch, J. & Irion, A. *The Psychology of Human Learning*. David McKay Co. 1952. Although now somewhat out of date, the book was a landmark in its time. The first three chapters plus the chapter on the law of effect are still worth reading.

Melton, A. (Ed.) *Categories of Human Learning*. Academic Press. 1965. A valuable book of contributed papers on various topics in learning. The chapters by David Grant and Gregory Kimble are "in depth" discussions of issues only touched on in this chapter. The concluding chapter by Melton is a useful discussion of the general issue of classification of types of learning.

Riley, D. *Discrimination Learning*. Allyn and Bacon, Inc. 1968. A modern, fairly high-level treatment of one of the most fundamental topics in the study of learning. Chapters 1 and 2 provide a basic understanding of concepts and terminology.

Smith, W. & Moore, J. *Conditioning and Instrumental Learning*. McGraw-Hill. 1966. A semi-programmed text covering the fundamentals. Especially useful for terminology.

Thorndike, E. L. *Human Learning*. The MIT Press. 1966. Thorndike was one of the founders of modern learning theory. This book represents a series of lectures designed to implement his ideas about learning in practical situations. The last two chapters on the evolution of learning form a background for present day educational psychology.

4
Conditions of
Learning and
Principles of
Practice

"I can't believe that!" said Alice.
"Can't you?" (the Queen said) "Try again: draw a long
breath and shut your eyes."

The simple principle, that behavior depends on its consequences, is apparent to almost everyone and, in fact, people are more or less successful in coping with their behavioral environment to the extent that they apply this law systematically in their contacts with others. Although we realize that teachers and parents are engaged in the control of behavior, it is perhaps less obvious that everyone is engaged in controlling behavior even if it is his own.

In order to control an individual's behavior, the principles of operant conditioning state quite clearly that we must provide the individual with a payoff for executing the desired responses. The likelihood that the responses we are interested in will recur depends on these consequences or payoffs. The difference between success and failure in applying this principle is usually the extent to which we are able to define, precisely, the behavior whose frequency of occurrence we wish to change and then reinforce approximations to this behavior. In other words, if we wait for the behavior we are interested in to appear full blown, it might never occur. What is required is that we reinforce approximations to the desired behavior and then continually modify the contingencies so that we reinforce only the approximations that are increasingly like the criterion or terminal behavior.

The Concept of Reinforcement

At the heart of successful behavior control is the concept of reinforcement. Recall from the previous chapter that a reinforcer is defined as anything that increases the frequency of an immediately preceding response. This definition suggests that the way to tell whether a given event is reinforcing is to make a direct test. We observe the frequency of a selected response. Then we make an event contingent on it and observe any change in the frequency of the response. If there is a change in frequency, we classify the event as reinforcing. If there is no change in the frequency of the response, the event is classified as nonreinforcing. (Some would say that reinforcers can either maintain or increase the frequency of a response; however, we shall define reinforcers as only those things that actually increase response frequency.)

The definition of reinforcement is circular because whether something is reinforcing is always determined after the fact. In other words, the definition allows us to conclude that any change in an individual's behavior is a function of some reinforcement. If, for instance, a child who has not previously reached for a toy now does so, then reaching for the toy must have been reinforced. To break out of this circularity we must go back to the way in which the term reinforcement is used in research done on Type 2 learning with animals.

In the study of animal behavior, a reinforcer is typically not determined after the fact. It is determined in advance, for example, by starving the animal if the reinforcement to be used is food. Here, we do not define some behavior that the animal makes and then consider food to be reinforcing because it increases the frequency of this behavior. In a typical Type 2 learning situation, we starve a pigeon until he weighs only 80% of what he normally does. This operation, deprivation of food, has made food a reinforcer for him. Thereafter, we can manipulate the presentation of food, properly timed, as an independent variable and we can demonstrate that a variety of behaviors, such as neck stretching and pecking at keys, are functions of this variable. Pigeons who are not hungry will not stretch their necks or peck keys because food is not reinforcing for them. A pigeon's neck-stretching behavior or a rat's bar-pressing behavior is controlled by giving him food when he pushes the bar or stretches his neck, but this only occurs because the animal is hungry.

To apply the principles of operant conditioning to human behavior, we determine reinforcers, not by manipulating the state of the organism but rather by finding out for what he will work. This is typically done by providing an individual with a choice from a number of alternative stimuli (for example, in the case of a child, "Which would you rather have, a peanut, chocolate, or a paper clip?"). We define what the individual would most like to have as a positive stimulus (we could also simply ask him to tell us without providing alternatives). The presentation of this stimulus we call reinforcement and its withdrawal we call punishment.

We could also attempt to establish a hierarchy of negative reinforcers by asking the individual such questions as: "What are you most afraid of?" "What would you least like to have?" We define things that the individual wants to avoid as negative stimuli. The presentation of such stimuli constitutes a form of punishment and their withdrawal is then negative reinforcement. Once we establish a hierarchy of reinforcers for an individual or group of individuals, we can proceed to manipulate them in order to affect behavior in systematic ways.

Modifying Behavior

Notice that what constitute positive and negative stimuli for an individual may not always be obvious. It may be the case, for example, that normal children prefer chocolate to peanuts and paper clips, but that retarded youngsters prefer the paper clips. It is important to be certain that we know what will work as reinforcers for individuals before beginning to modify their behavior in any situation. Once we have determined the reinforcing stimuli, the next step is to define the behavior that we want the individual to display. That is, we need to define criterion behavior—what we want the organism to do when we are done with him. Finally, we determine what his present behavior is so that we have a basis for comparison.

Not only may food, money, praise, gold stars, pats on the back, and so forth be used as positive reinforcers, but also high probability behaviors can be used to reinforce low probability behaviors. This means that we can use a behavior that the individual makes with considerable frequency as a means of reinforcing a behavior that he makes less frequently. For instance, we might make problem solving in arithmetic contingent on the opportunity to play a game or to run around the room. The real task in most behavior modification work is to determine exactly what reinforcers an individual will work for so that we can use them to control the emission of responses that we want him to make.

The application of principles from operant conditioning to the modification of behavior suggests that we provide frequent reinforcement. If we reinforce only very occasionally, the behavior usually degenerates and ultimately disappears altogether. In fact, just as we can use reinforcers to increase the frequency of desirable behaviors, we can withhold reinforcers to decrease the frequency of undesirable behaviors.

Another way of decreasing the frequency of undesirable behaviors is to increase the probability of incompatible behaviors. If, for example, we want a child to stop running around the room, we might simultaneously extinguish (not reinforce) running around the room and reinforce standing in one place or sitting down. Since the two behaviors are incompatible and since we manipulate reinforcement and extinction simultaneously, we are able to change behavior more effectively than if we simply applied extinction or reinforcement separately.

Another principle suggested by our model for Type 2 learning is that we must provide reinforcement immediately after the response has been produced. The longer we wait before providing the organism with the reinforcing event, the more likely it is that other behaviors will occur in the intervening time and be strengthened instead.

Training

Recall that, in defining reinforcement, we also defined a concept of punishment. According to our definition, punishment is either the withdrawal of a positive stimulus or the presentation of a negative stimulus. Defined in this way, punishment can be an extremely effective tool to use in showing an individual what not to do. An example of this is the case in which we have trained a rat to press a bar. We now want to train him to press the bar when a light is on and not to press it when the light is off. Ordinarily, we might simply withhold reinforcement when the light is off. However, we could also shock the rat for pressing the bar when the light is off.

To take a more complicated situation, suppose we want to teach our rat to press a bar for food when a light is on but to turn a wheel for food when the light is off. Presenting a shock to the rat through the bar when the light is off makes it quite likely he will stop bar pressing, at least for awhile. And it also makes it likely that he will do other things such as moving the wheel. We could, of course, extinguish the response of pressing the bar when the light is off (discrimination training). However, establishment of a discrimination typically requires more time when extinction procedures are used than when punishment is employed. At the same time, there are some potentially hazardous consequences of using punishment that we shall presently consider.

Many professional animal trainers (as well as parents, for that matter) utilize punishment to a much greater extent than individuals trained on principles of operant conditioning, especially to eliminate undesirable responses. But, though professional trainers use punishment, they never use it alone. When a trainer uses punishment, he usually does so in conjunction with praise or reward. For example, given a horse who periodically rears and frightens its rider, a trainer may deal with the horse by striking it behind the ears with his hand as it rears. When the horse drops down on all four legs he is patted and praised. Or, if the horse does not stand still when his rider wants him to stand still, the trainer may suggest jerking sharply on the bit and saying, "stand." When the horse stands, he is praised and patted. Applying these techniques consistently over time often results in the elimination of the undesirable response.

The same techniques are used in training dogs in obedience school. A dog can be trained to heel, for example, by attaching a leash to a choke collar. The choke collar is a device that cuts off the dog's wind quite sharply and painfully when pressure is applied to it. In the training situation, the trainer begins walking and the dog starts to follow. If the dog does not keep up or does not follow to begin with, the trainer jerks the leash and tells the dog to "heel." If the dog gets too far ahead he is also jerked back beside the trainer and told to "heel." In each case the dog is praised for making the correct response, namely, for remaining beside the trainer.

We have principles of training that are based on subtle combinations of reward and punishment and we have principles of behavior modification that grow out of operant conditioning or Type 2 learning. The major difference between these two sets of principles is that the ones arising in the context of the professional animal trainer embody a combination of reward and punishment that have been developed by trial and error, often in the context of a master apprentice relationship. Those that derive from Type 2 learning follow principles developed in the laboratory and capitalize almost solely on the use of reinforcement.

One reason often given for the use of reinforcement alone rather than a combination of reinforcement and punishment is the undesirable side effects of punishment. We often hear, for instance, that punishment can arouse fear and anxiety in the organism and that these undesirable states in fact become responses that are associated with other stimulus events. Such is the case, we suppose, when the child comes to fear his father because the father punishes him for crying or for not eating at the table. The father has become an aversive stimulus, a feared individual. (On the anecdotal level, however, it is interesting to note that many animals who have been trained using a combination of reward and punishment are devoted to their trainers.)

In the above example, the father has become a secondary or conditioned reinforcer. Secondary reinforcers are stimulus events that have been paired with primary reinforcers and take on reinforcing properties because of their contiguous occurrence with one another (Type 1 learning). Secondary reinforcers can be either positive or negative. Although in the previous case they were negative, they can also be effective in the positive sense. If, for example, we wish to train a dog to put his nose to a doorknob, we might begin by pairing the presentation of food with a click emitted by a small hand clicker. It is important in this operation that we present the click first and immediately follow it by the food (again, Type 1 learning). Eventually the click becomes a signal for the food. Thereafter, we can use the click to tell the dog, so to speak, that he has emitted an appropriate behavior when he is physically removed from us so that we cannot present him with food and, moreover, when the responses involved in eating the food would be incompatible with the behavior we are trying to condition.

To proceed with our example, we now wait until the dog turns toward the doorknob, at which point we press the clicker. As the dog walks toward the doorknob, we press the clicker again and, finally, we press the clicker when he puts his nose on the knob. Eventually, of course, after having progressed through the chain of behavior and being reinforced solely by the clicks, we must present the dog with the primary reinforcer, namely, food. But the point is that the behavioral chain was established by the use of the secondary reinforcer, which was, in this case, positive.

Principles of Practice

Principles of practice are intuitions about the determinants of behavior. As such, they have two origins. In one sense they are common knowledge and are employed more or less systematically by individuals in our society. On the other hand, such principles are also derived from a body of knowledge in experimental psychology. In some cases, the principles are not identical and, indeed, there is no reason why they should be. Presumably, the difference between the two levels of principles lies in the greater generality embodied in those principles based on the science of psychology although, in either case, application of these principles is at present more an art than a science.

Notice that what we have referred to as principles of practice is not the same as principles of instruction. In Chapter 1, we defined principles of instruction as prescriptive statements based on descriptive laws that are constructed to explain behavioral phenomena. In that chapter, we argued that, because we do not have any well-established descriptive laws for human behavior, there are no well-formulated principles of instruction.

Although principles of behavior modification may seem to be principles of instruction (since presumably they are based on descriptive statements for Type 2 learning), they are not. The reason they are not is that almost all descriptive statements for Type 2 learning come from research with animals (particularly pigeons and white rats). If we were to set ourselves the task of training such animals then we would have some basis for formulating principles of instruction. When we generalize descriptive statements from Type 2 learning to human behavior we no longer have principles of instruction in the sense in which we have used the term here.

However, principles of instruction can be supplanted by principles of practice and, indeed, this is done every day by individuals who are concerned with changing the behavior of others. We suppose that the principles of psychology can be ultimately developed to the point where systematic prescriptive statements can be constructed from them. Until that time, however, principles of practice as formulated by practitioners and psychologists must function as approximations to well-defined ways for controlling behavior.

Summary

In Chapter 1, we defined a process called school learning. This process is complex and can be described on several levels. We assumed that the major independent variable in school learning is the curriculum, and the major dependent variable is achievement. Principles of instruction are then based on descriptive statements linking these two variables. At the same time, we have principles of practice for school learning. For classes surely meet and children are taught and very little of this happens because of what we have termed "principles of instruction." What, if anything, can we say about the relationship between these two sets of principles? In the last chapter of this book, we shall argue that principles of practice are based on an intuitive knowledge of macroscopic variables, and principles of instruction are formulated from knowledge gained by the systematic manipulation of macroscopic variables.

By the term "macroscopic variables," we mean variables that predict change in a "real life" phenomenon such as schooling. These are to be contrasted with microscopic variables formulated to explain the behavior of "idealized" phenomena. Perhaps an analogy would be helpful. In physics, the behavior of a gas can be "explained" on two levels. On the macroscopic level, we can use pressure, volume, and temperature as the major variables that control the behavior of a gas. On the microscopic level, we can suppose a gas actually consists of very small particles, like billiard balls, which have a certain mass and velocity. This is called the kinetic theory and we can describe the behavior of gases under various conditions based on the supposed behavior of these hypothetical particles.

The point of the analogy, as far as we are concerned, is that human behavior can be described on two levels. Principles of practice are effective in dealing with the behavior of individuals in practical situations and are based on macroscopic rather than microscopic variables. They are, in other words, independent variables determined by observing the behavior of an individual or group of individuals under conditions that are subject to manipulation by other individuals. As such, they are not based on any model or hypothetical structure that can be used to explain the changes that they create. At the same time, a theoretical concern with behavioral change would dictate a model such as the kinetic theory model in the case of gases from which we could derive or predict observed changes in behavior.

Unfortunately, we have very few principles of instruction for human behavior at the moment. They must await progress in the laboratory description of human behavior and, in particular, the kind of behavior used to acquire knowledge. Stated another way, we are unable to explain the conditions for effective school learning without a precise definition of the behaviors that comprise it and the stimuli that control it.

Suggested Readings

Cohen, J. Operant Behavior and Operant Conditioning. *Eyewitness Series in Psychology.* Rand McNally and Co. 1969. A paperback with excellent examples of techniques for modifying behavior.

Logan, F. & Wagner, A. *Reward and Punishment.* Allyn and Bacon. 1965. A paperback stressing work with animals. Chapter 3, on incentives, is the point of departure for many applications from the laboratory to "real life" situations.

Millenson, J. R. *Principles of Behavioral Analysis.* Macmillan. 1969. A number of chapters in this thorough introduction to the analysis of behavior are worthwhile. Chapter 1 gives a good overview of the Zeitgeist within which principles of operant conditioning are applied.

Nuttin, J. & Greenwald, A. *Reward and Punishment in Human Learning.* Academic Press. 1968. A physiological interpretation of reward and punishment to be contrasted with the discussion by Postman in *Psychology in the Making.* The book is on a fairly high level.

Postman, L. Rewards and Punishment in Human Learning. In *Psychology in the Making.* L. Postman (Ed.) Alfred A. Knopf, Inc. 1964. An excellent historical review and critique of basic concepts.

Reese, E. The Analysis of Human Operant Behavior. *Introduction to Psychology: A Self Selection Textbook.* William C. Brown Co. 1966. A good introduction to the various uses of principles of operant conditioning to control human behavior, particularly among the mentally ill.

Skinner, B. F. *Science and Human Behavior.* The Free Press. 1953. The basic statement of the "operant conditioning position" by its founding father. Sections I, V, and VI are particularly provocative.

Stephens, J. M. *The Psychology of Classroom Learning.* Holt, Rinehart and Winston. 1965. Chapter 5 is a good introductory level presentation of principles of behavior management for the classroom teacher.

Ullman, L. & Krasner, L. *Case Studies in Behavior Modification.* Holt, Rinehart and Winston. 1965. A compendium of examples on the uses of conditioning principles to modify pathological behavior.

Ulrich, R., Stachnik, T., & Mabry, J. *Control of Human Behavior.* Scott, Foresman and Co. 1966. A book of readings covering most applications of operant conditioning principles to human behavior.

5

Conceptual Behavior

"Are we nearly there?" Alice managed to pant out at last.
"Nearly there!" the Queen repeated. "Why, we passed
it ten minutes ago!"

Conceptual behavior can be described as the occurrence of a common response to a class of objects or events, where we can be assured that this common response is not due to stimulus generalization. The basic operation in learning concepts is discrimination, by which we break down generalizations among similar things and thus learn to differentiate among them. Suppose, for example, that we take a young child for a walk and a rabbit appears; we point to it and say, "rabbit," after which the child may say "rabbit." On proceeding further, another rabbit appears and this time the child spontaneously says, "rabbit," after which we praise him for his correct behavior. At subsequent times, the child continues to respond with the word "rabbit" to instances of this concept. However, by chance, we discover that the child thinks each instance he sees is the same rabbit appearing over and over again. Clearly, there is a sense in which he does not know the concept. We take account of this by saying that the child must make a common response to each instance of a concept, and in addition he must also be able to identify each instance as different from the others.

Conceptual learning consists of forming associations between particular objects or events and a common response. As a result of the acquisition of these associations, stimulus generalization appears. This generalization must be dissolved by a process of discrimination training so that each stimulus can be independently identified in its own right. After this training, the individual must be able to respond to the stimuli as if they were the same but now he can also differentiate among them. Conceptual behavior reaches its end point, so to speak, when a new instance that previously has not been experienced can be labeled appropriately with the common response.

Concepts

In the simplest sense, a concept is usually understood to be a grouping of things or, perhaps more correctly, a partitioning of things into positive and negative classes. Positive classes consist of those things that are instances of the concept and negative classes consist of those things that are not. Concepts can be described in this sense by means of dimensions and attributes. This is accomplished by partitioning objects and events into categories or dimensions, by which we mean that an object or event is described in terms of certain more general characteristics. Thus, we might decide that some particular object has the dimensions of color, shape, and size. Once we have chosen a series of dimensions we assign values to them. In the case of color, we might choose red and green. In the case of size, we might choose large and small, and for shape, triangle and square. Stimulus dimensions and their values are the means by which we discriminate objects from one another. The particular values that dimensions have in a given instance are called attributes.

A rule is used to specify which attributes are necessary for the definition of a concept; it specifies how the attributes are to be combined. For example, we might choose the rule "all black things that are triangles" or we might choose the rule "all black things." The rule determines which attributes are necessary for an object to be an instance of a concept. Those instances that contain the necessary or critical attributes are positive instances, and those that do not contain these attributes are negative instances.

There are various kinds of rules that can be used to specify the way in which attributes are combined to define a concept. We shall consider three of these. The first and simplest rule is affirmation. By this we mean that one attribute is chosen as criterial or distinguishing for the concept. Black might be an attribute; or triangular, or square, or toothy, or furry, or some other value characteristic of a stimulus. The second rule is conjunction. Here we mean the combination of two or more attributes. Examples would be large squares, or red triangles, or furry animals with big ears. The third rule, which we encounter less frequently in our everyday lives, is disjunction. This is an and/or combination of attributes. We might decide, for example, that all black things and/or all triangles, constitute the concept we are interested in studying or communicating.

The idea that a concept can be described by means of a rule and a collection of attributes leads to many arbitrary concepts in the sense that they have no particular logical status. We might use the preceding procedure to decide, for example, that cherries and steak constitute a concept because both are red, juicy, and edible. The above procedure does not in itself provide a means for deciding which concepts are meaningful in the sense of our everyday experience and which are purely constructions of our imagination.

Acquisition

In general, concepts are acquired by two more or less distinct learning procedures. The first of these procedures we shall call reception learning. Here positive and negative instances of a concept are presented to individuals and they must learn to identify these correctly. By positive instances, as stated earlier, we mean objects or events that contain the criterial attributes of the concept as defined by the rule that applies to it. Negative instances, on the other hand, may contain some of the attributes of the concept but not all. In reception learning, the individual is presented with one instance at a time and must guess whether it is a positive or negative instance. Immediately on guessing, we supply him with information about the appropriateness of his response, after which we give him another instance and he again guesses whether it is positive or negative. In this fashion, we continue through the entire population of positive and negative instances, more than once if necessary, until the subject can, without error, correctly identify those instances that represent the concept defined by the rule.

A second means of studying concept acquisition is called selection learning. Here, the subject is exposed to the entire set of instances (both positive and negative). The teacher or the experimenter than selects an instance and tells the subject that it is positive. The subject must then choose another positive instance from the total population of stimuli. After he has chosen, he is informed about the appropriateness of his choice, and, on the basis of that information he chooses another instance. The major difference between the reception and selection learning methods of acquiring concepts is that, in the latter case, we are able to examine the strategies employed by individuals in acquiring concepts. That is, we are able to observe the choices that they make on the basis of the information we supply regarding the correctness or incorrectness of their previous choices.

It should be apparent that what we are calling concept acquisition can also be labeled, perhaps more appropriately, concept utilization. What we have been describing is not the initial formation or acquisition of concepts as much as it is the utilization of concepts already known. The situation might even be classified as a problem-solving task where the individual must guess what it is that the teacher or experimenter has in mind.

Concept utilization should be contrasted with true concept acquisition, in which the individual acquires a concept for the first time. In this latter case, we might ask about the conditions under which individuals acquire the concept of triangle, or number, or electron, or mammal. Much less is known about the acquisition of concepts than about their utilization in problem-solving situations.

Evaluation

To determine whether an individual has acquired a concept, we must construct tasks to test for it. Of course, during the process of acquisition, we can record an individual's responses and plot a graph of performance over trials, as described in Chapter 3. Such a "performance curve" gives us information about the acquisition of particular responses but does not tell us in what sense the individual has acquired the rules used to generate concept instances. In order to determine whether a concept has been acquired in this latter sense, we must use additional tasks. To test for concept acquisition more generally, we must employ a second performance situation that is related to the conditions of initial acquisition. An example of this is presented in Figure 5–1.

Here we see that the individual's first task is to learn that the concept is "large." The rule is one of simple affirmation. The individual is presented with large squares and small squares, large triangles and small triangles. Positive instances are only those things that are large. After performing correctly in such a situation, we might want to know what it is that individuals have learned. One way to ask this question is by presenting a second task, as illustrated in Figure 5-1. Here, the second task actually has two forms. In one form, we have changed the positive

First task   Second task

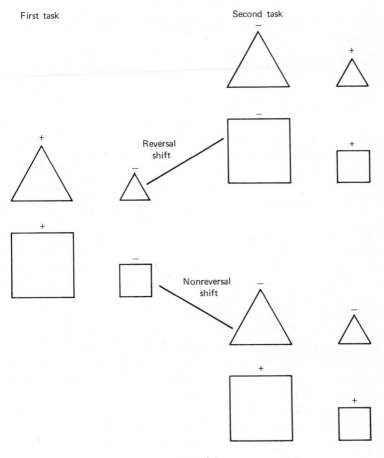

FIGURE 5-1
Reversal and nonreversal shifts.

instances from large to small. In the other form, we have changed the positive instances from large to square. The first form is referred to as a reversal shift and the second is a nonreversal shift.

When we present the second task to very young children, it is typically easier for them to learn the nonreversal shift than the reversal shift. However, after the children are old enough to use language, they find the reversal shift easier than the nonreversal shift. Moreover, college sophomores and adults also find the reversal shift easier than the nonreversal shift. The question that arises is: What have individuals learned in the first situation that makes either the reversal or the nonreversal shift easier for them as a second task?

One hypothesis that has been advanced to account for performance in the second task in Figure 5-1 is that after individuals have acquired a language they mediate their behavior by means of verbal labels. In other words, they verbally describe the rule that is used to define the positive and negative instances. In the case of the first task in Figure 5-1, the rule is simple affirmation, so the individual might label the concept as "large," thus defining size as the dimension containing the critical attributes. In the reversal shift condition, the individual discovers that size is still the relevant dimension but that positive instances have been changed from large to small. For example, he might say to himself, "small but not large."

In the case of the nonreversal shift, no such verbal label will suffice, for here one of the formerly positive instances is still a positive instance, namely, the large square. On the other hand, the large triangle is no longer correct, so the rule has changed not only the attribute but also the dimension. The dimension that is now correct is not size but shape. This task is typically more difficult for individuals if they have labeled the appropriate dimension in the first task (for example, individuals would have to say "square, not large"). Such labeling is unavailable to very young children who have not yet acquired language. It is interesting to note that animals typically find the nonreversal shift easier than the reversal shift, thus substantiating the notion that it is language that serves to mediate performance between the two task situations.

We can also use two tasks to determine whether the subject has learned what we suppose he has learned during acquisition. Figure 5-2 illustrates a situation where the task consists of learning to associate numbers with colored geometric forms.

After an individual has learned to respond correctly in this task, we can ask whether he is responding to colored shapes, or simply to color or shape alone. For example, the individual might be responding totally on the basis of color and not at all on the basis of form. Or, he might be responding totally on the basis of form. In either case his performance will be correct. Said another way, there are two independent variables (dimensions) in each stimulus and they vary in a completely confounded manner. By studying performance during acquisition, we are not able to determine whether the individual is attending to one or both of these stimulus dimensions in performing correctly.

In order to understand what has been learned, a second task is needed, in which some individuals are given only uncolored geometric forms

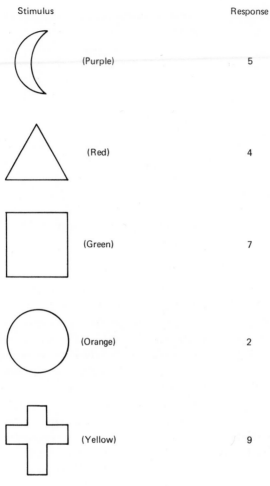

Stimulus   Response

(Purple)   5

(Red)   4

(Green)   7

(Orange)   2

(Yellow)   9

FIGURE 5-2
Learning task with confounded variables.

and other individuals are given simply colored chips. If an individual has learned to respond on the basis of color, he should do better when given colored chips than when he is given uncolored triangles and squares. If, on the other hand, he has learned to respond to geometric form, his performance should be better when he is given form as a stimulus than when he is given color.

A third example of the use of two tasks to evaluate first task acquisition is illustrated in Figure 5-3. Here the stimulus population is defined by

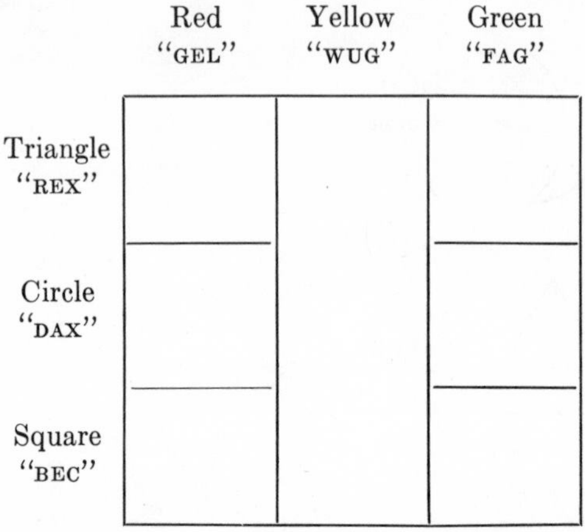

	Red "GEL"	Yellow "WUG"	Green "FAG"
Triangle "REX"			
Circle "DAX"			
Square "BEC"			

FIGURE 5-3
Concept learning task with two independent
dimensions.

two dimensions—color and shape. Color has three attributes—yellow, green, and red; shape also has three attributes—triangles, circles, and squares. In addition, each attribute on each of the dimensions is labeled by a nonsense syllable. These nonsense syllables are indicated in Figure 5-3 in the margins. The concept acquisition task presented to the subject is one in which he must learn to correctly label a geometric form. Thus, for example, we present him with a red triangle and tell him that it is a GELREX. A green square is then a FAGBEC and so on (reception learning). We could, of course, present all nine geometric forms and their appropriate labels and thereby teach the individual the whole population of stimulus items. On the other hand, we might teach just a portion of the stimulus objects and see whether the individual has learned the others as well. Thus, we might teach the diagonal cells in Figure 5-3 in the first task, and in a second task ask whether the individual can respond correctly to instances represented by the other cells. If the individual can correctly label stimuli in the other cells in the second task, we say that he has learned a rule. The rule that he has learned in this case is the way in which the attributes are labeled by the nonsense words.

Instruction

The example illustrated in Figure 5-3 suggests that in most concept acquisition situations the task for the teacher or the individual attempting to communicate a concept is to choose some representative set of instances that most effectively communicate the concept. If the concept is complicated so that the stimulus population is large, teaching the whole universe of instances if often a difficult if not impossible task. The question of instructional strategies therefore arises.

This question is not unlike the part-whole problem that has been studied in psychology and education for some time. We are asking what the minimal (sub) set of stimuli is to which we must expose an individual to ensure that he knows the total set of stimuli to which we want him to respond correctly. In the previous example, we could teach just the geometric forms and labels represented by the diagonal cells. But notice that this would not be an optimal strategy in the sense that the individual would not know what the appropriate label was for an instance represented by any other cell on the table. In other words, given that a red triangle is a GELREX, the subject does not know whether GEL refers to red or to triangle. In order to communicate sufficient information of this sort, we need to present him with at least one other cell in the table, one that contains either red or triangle. He can then determine that REX is the appropriate label for triangle, not GEL.

Clearly, many of the concepts that we have been considering are not of the sort ordinarily encountered by individuals in their natural environment or in the course of school learning. To extend our analysis to such concepts, we must define a population of relevant concept instances. Since it is often difficult to define the criterial attributes for concepts like democracy, gene, force, or mammal, we usually tackle the problem of defining such concepts by means of the behaviors that can be used to determine a knowledge of them. Thus, for example, we say that the concept of gene is defined by all those things that biologists and teachers of biology tell us people should be able to do when they know the concept.

This approach to the definition of a concept results in a large domain of criterion behaviors or test items. To the extent that we can dimensionalize (describe) these behaviors, we can interpret them by means of rules and attributes. That is, we can define dimensions and attributes along these dimensions and then use rules to combine the attributes according to the idea for the concept we have in mind. However, more often we have no good idea of the dimensions underlying a population of test behaviors. Therefore, we must resort to randomly sampling from among the possible items that we can use to test a knowledge of what we are trying to teach.

Stated another way, the usual approach to teaching concepts is to sample some set of behaviors that are used to test knowledge and then to teach these behaviors in the course of instruction. During testing, we sample another portion of the population of behaviors as well as the portion used during acquisition. If an individual can respond correctly to items that he has not seen during training as well as to those he has seen, we infer that he has understood the concept represented by the population of items.

The Role of Language

For human beings, words and concepts are inextricably bound together. It is often difficult to even think about some concepts without immediately associating a verbal label with them. Not only is it the case that many concepts are identified primarily by means of verbal labels, but it is also true, especially in everyday experience, that some concepts such as justice and culture are defined almost exclusively by the verbal environments in which they occur. A good many concepts are defined not by means of attributes and dimensions but rather by the associations or relations that their verbal labels have with other verbal labels in some defined population of discourse. Concepts in this latter sense consist of the meanings of words.

One means of describing a knowledge of such concepts is to try to arrange the words whose meanings represent them in a hierarchical structure. An example of such a structure for the concept of power in physics is presented in Figure 5-4.

To construct such a structure we begin with the concept of power and ask what concepts are logically prerequisite to it. The answer to this question leads to the concepts represented at the second level of the structure. We then take each of these concepts and ask the same question, ultimately arriving at the primitive or most basic concepts. Such an analysis is not without its difficulties but it has the virtue of pointing out possible hierarchical dependencies between concepts that must be taken into account in sequencing instruction. Thus, we might suppose that in order to be able to understand the concept of power we must first understand the concepts of work and time. And to understand each of these concepts, we must in turn understand those below it. Notice that some concepts recur as "primitives" several times at different points in the structure. Presumably these concepts are the most fundamental to a knowledge of the rest of the structure.

The greatest danger in using such a structure is that we forget that individuals may disagree with one another. There is no reason to suppose, for example, that all physicists would generate the structure for

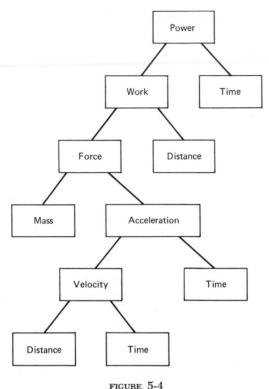

FIGURE 5-4
Hierarchical structure for the concept of power in physics.

power illustrated in Figure 5-4. Nor would all biologists generate the same structure for the concept of gene. In order for such an approach to be fruitfully employed it is necessary to make the individual himself a sampling variable. This means that we must begin by defining a population of individuals and then sample from this population, using their responses to construct some composite or representative structure.

Summary

The range of variation in conceptual behavior is large. On one hand, we have concepts being utilized to solve problems by the rules of affirmation, conjunction, and disjunction. Conceptual behavior in this sense consists of learning the ways in which attributes are combined in order to define a particular, unique or common category of response. On the other hand, we have the formulation of theories and complex ideas in science and literature. In this latter case, conceptual behavior consists of the development and utilization of ideas in relation to one another, and the formulation of propositions. Propositions lead to prediction and are at the heart of conceptual behavior in subject matter and school learning. Thus, for example, the proposition that all whales are mammals leads to the prediction that female whales suckle their young. Conceptual behavior in the sense of propositions allows one to formulate complex networks of ideas which, in turn, lead to other ideas, as well as the ways in which these ideas can be tested by experience.

It is not so much that the psychologist has been unsuccessful in describing conceptual behavior in the latter sense, but that he has not devoted a great deal of effort to it. Of course it is possible that the problem is so enormous and that our tools so inadequate to the task that there is no use even beginning. However, it is more likely that success breeds success, and in those areas where the psychologist has been successful he continues to work. Thus, we know a fair amount about conceptual behavior involving concepts that are defined by means of simple stimulus dimensions and much less about concepts defined by the meanings of words.

It is undoubtedly true that some models for fundamental human processes, uncovered in studying conceptual behavior, generalize across stimuli and tasks. However, the complexity of stimuli and tasks found in school learning may mask important common aspects. We need to devote more attention to the study of concepts as they are found in everyday experience and in the academic disciplines. Only then will it be possible to formulate adequate principles of instruction for conceptual behavior.

Suggested Readings

Berlyne, D. E. *Structure and Direction in Thinking.* John Wiley and Sons. 1965. Chapter 1 is a good review of the "associationist" position for studying behavior. Chapters 2–9, while somewhat technical in places, form the basis for an associationist analysis of conceptual behavior.

Bourne, L. E. *Human Conceptual Behavior.* Allyn and Bacon Inc. 1966. An excellent survey of research and methodology. The whole book (a paperback) can be profitably read by the beginner.

Bruner, J. et al. *Studies in Cognitive Growth.* John Wiley and Sons. 1967. A somewhat uneven book of research studies whose point of view is largely derived from Piaget. Chapters 1 and 2 are the most valuable.

Hunt, E. B. *Concept Learning: An Information Processing Problem.* John

Wiley and Sons. 1965. A fairly high-level book. Chapters 1–3 contain the basic argument for those interested in uses of computers as analogs for studying behavior.

Hunt, J. McV. *Intelligence and Experience.* The Ronald Press. A valuable book that attempts to "bridge the gap" between intelligence and conceptual behavior. The latter chapters are devoted to a discussion of Piaget. For our purposes Chapters 1–4 on the nature of intelligence and development are probably the most useful.

Klausmeier, H. & Harris, C. (Eds.) *Analyses of Concept Learning.* Academic Press. 1966. A book of readings with wide ranging content. Although every article deserves attention, a unique feature of this book is the analysis of concepts in subject matters contained in Chapters 13–16.

Phillips, J. L. *The Origins of Intellect—Piaget's Theory.* W. H. Freeman. 1965. An overview of one of today's major theories about conceptual behavior. The book is written with an eye to the teacher; it is a paperback and should be read in its entirety.

Staats, A. W. *Learning, Language, and Cognition.* Holt, Rinehart and Winston, Inc. 1968. Chapter 9 contains an analysis of concept learning from the operant conditioning point of view. Other relevant information regarding conceptual behavior can be obtained by skimming the extensive table of contents.

6

Transfer

"That's a great deal to make one word mean," Alice said in a thoughtful tone.
"When I make a word do a lot of work like that," said Humpty Dumpty, "I always pay it extra."

We seldom learn without being affected by past experience. This simple statement contains the basic idea of transfer, a fundamental concept in the study of human learning. Transfer is also at the heart of most educational programs in the sense that we presume that students have the ability to transfer what they have learned from one situation to another.

Transfer as a concept in the study of human learning can be viewed in at least three ways. First, we can think of it as an effect. Transfer in this sense is either positive, negative, or zero. A positive transfer effect means that the results of previous learning enhance or increase performance in a new situation. A negative transfer effect means that prior performance contributes a decrement to performance in a new situation. And by zero transfer effects we mean that performance on a new task seems to be unrelated to performance on a prior task.

Transfer can also be viewed as a process, a means of carrying what we have learned from one situation to another. If we view transfer as a process then all transfer is positive. That is to say, even when we observe negative transfer effects, the effects can be attributed to the results of prior learning. It is only when we have a zero transfer effect that there is no positive transfer in the process sense.

TABLE 6-1
Basic Transfer Design

Group 1	Learn A	Learn B
Group 2		Learn B

Transfer can also be seen as a class of designs for describing behavior. In order to understand transfer in this sense, consider the diagram in Table 6-1.

Table 6-1 illustrates the basic two-groups design presented in Chapter 2. There is an experimental group and a control group. The experimental group receives both tasks A and B, whereas the control group receives only task B. We compare the performance of the two groups on task B. If the experimental group performs better than the control group, we say that this is due to the effects of task A. As we pointed out in Chapter 2, however, simply because the experimental group performs better than the control group on task B is no assurance that this performance increase is due to the previous experience in task A. The increase in performance in the second situation could be due to a variety of factors and we have only isolated one of these. To understand whether the performance in task B is truly influenced by task A we need to add additional groups, as illustrated in Table 6-2.

TABLE 6-2
Basic Transfer Design with
Additional Groups

Group 1	Learn A	Learn B
Group 2		Learn B
Group 3	Learn A_1	Learn B
Group 4	Learn A_2	Learn B
Group 5	Learn A	Learn B_1
Group 6	Learn A	Learn B_2

We might, for example, break up task A into components and present each separately in order to find out what aspect of A contributes to the observed differences in performance. Thus, as was mentioned previously, we might try variations such as different foreign languages when we are concerned with the transfer between two languages. Or we might present just the grammar in one case and just vocabulary in the other. We could also try to isolate various aspects of the second task, B, to determine whether just part of B or all of it is affected by previous experience with A. The point is that two groups are seldom sufficient to determine the sources of transfer between one task and another.

Measures of Transfer

In order to assess specific transfer effects from a first to a second task, we compare performance between the experimental and control groups on the second task. A number of measures are available for describing the difference between the experimental and control groups in a transfer design. We shall consider three of these.

Our first measure of transfer is obtained by dividing the difference in performance between the experimental and the control group, multiplied by 100 times the control group's performance (that is, percent transfer $= (E - C)/C \times 100$). We can also measure the percent transfer between two tasks by dividing the difference in performance between the experimental and control group multiplied by 100 times the total performance possible on the second task, minus the control group's performance on that task or $(E - C)/(T - C) \times 100$. Neither of these two measures of transfer is without difficulties. In the first case, we can achieve positive transfer scores greater than one hundred percent, while the maximum value of negative transfer is minus 100 percent. On the second task, maximum positive transfer is 100 percent, but the maximum negative transfer is minus infinity.

A more balanced, though less sensitive, measure of transfer is one in which we divide the difference in performance between the experimental and control groups by the experimental group's performance plus the control group's performance, multiplied by 100, $(E - C)/(E + C) \times 100$. This latter measure expresses the ratio of the difference between the experimental and control group scores to the sum of these scores. The measure is symmetrically distributed about zero and has a maximum positive transfer of 100 percent and maximum negative transfer of minus 100 percent.

Specific Transfer Effects

We shall now consider a learning situation in which the independent variables that contribute to between task differences can be fairly well described. In particular, suppose we have a "paired associates" situation in which individuals must learn to associate two sets of things with one another. These two sets might be nonsense syllables paired with nonsense syllables, words paired with nonsense syllables, words paired with numbers, or geometric forms paired with words. Any such configuration will do. In a task of this sort, we call the first element the stimulus and the second element the response.

Some independent variables that can affect transfer from one paired associate task to another are (1) response meaningfulness, (2) degree of original (first task) learning, (3) stimulus similarity, and (4) response similarity. We can manipulate each of these independent variables singly or together and ask about their effect on second task performance.

By response meaningfulness we mean how familiar the response items are to the learner. We can assume, for example, that nonsense syllables such as KEZ are reasonably unfamiliar to the average learner. On the other hand, a nonsense syllable such as KIL is considerably more meaningful, as is a nonsense syllable such as DUZ.

Degree of original learning simply refers to how much practice individuals are allowed on the first task. This can vary from almost no original learning to considerable overlearning, in which individuals practice beyond criterion performance (for example, no errors for ten consecutive trials).

Stimulus and response similarity refer to the extent to which individuals respond alike to elements on the stimulus or response side of the paired associate task. This similarity may be defined in a variety of ways. It is the task of the investigator in any transfer situation to obtain some measure of degree of similarity beforehand so that he can vary the independent variables which represent it.

The typical effect of stimulus and response similarity on second task performance is summarized in Figure 6-1. The A-B in the center of Figure 6-1 refers to a task in which the subject must learn to associate B_1 with A_1, B_2 with A_2, and so forth through a list of several items. The outer ring of boxes in the figure indicates types of other tasks These tasks vary from one that is identical to the first task (A-B) to one that involves totally different stimuli and responses (C-D). Between these extremes, we have tasks in which only the stimulus has been

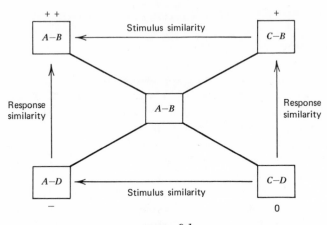

FIGURE 6-1
Transfer effects for variations in stimulus and response similarity.

changed (*C-B*) and tasks in which only the response has been changed (*A-D*). The arrows in the figure refer to changing either responses or stimuli along some defined dimension of similarity (for example, dimensions of stimulus and response generalization).

The diagram in Figure 6-1 indicates that we can expect maximum positive transfer when the two tasks are identical (*A-B*, *A-B*), and that we can expect zero transfer when the two tasks are totally unrelated to one another (*A-B*, *C-D*). Between these two extremes, we find that, if we leave the stimulus the same in the two tasks, we have negative transfer (*A-B*, *A-D*). This is because the individual must learn new responses to old stimuli. In the process of doing this, the old responses that have been associated with the stimuli in the first task get in the way, so to speak, of the associations he is trying to form. We refer to this latter situation as response competition. Response competition must be overcome in order for second task performance to reach criterion. On the other hand, if we change stimuli and leave responses the same in the two tasks (*A-B*, *C-B*), we generally observe positive transfer. That is because the old stimuli are no longer present to elicit competing responses and because responses on the two tasks are the same, thus permitting past learning of responses to be utilized.

We can now expand our analysis of between task relationships in the paired associate situation to take account of degree of first task or original learning and response meaningfulness. To do this, we shall suppose that the actual learning of any paired associate list consists of several component processes.

First, we suppose that, in order to learn a pair of items, an individual must begin by learning the responses because the task usually requires the production of responses in order for behavior to be scored. For example, we are usually required to say the responses out loud or write them down when the stimulus is presented.

Second, in a typical paired associate task an individual must form forward associations. He must, in other words, form associations between those things that are labeled stimuli and those things that are labeled responses, or, as is usually the case, those on the left and those on the right. Finally, he learns backward associations—associations between responses and stimuli. We suppose that this is done in the process of practice. Thus, in practicing the association A-B, A-B, A-B, we learn associations between B and A as well as between A and B.

The effect of these three processes on transfer performance is illustrated in Table 6-3. Notice that, when the two task situations are identical, each of the processes contributes positively and the overall transfer effect is positive. On the other hand, if we let the responses remain and change the stimuli in the two tasks, we have a positive contribution due to response learning, a zero contribution from forward associations, and a negative contribution from backward associations. The third row in Table 6-3 indicates that if the stimuli in the two tasks are the same and the responses are different, response learning can contribute nothing to performance. Forward associations, however, contribute negatively since any associations that are learned in the first task will compete with the associations to be acquired in the second task. Backward associations contribute nothing, so the overall transfer effect is negative. Finally, the fourth row in Table 6-3 illustrates the case in which we have two distinct tasks. Here, the stimuli and responses in the two tasks

TABLE 6-3

Component Process Analysis of Specific Transfer Effects
in Paired Associates Learning

Task	Response Learning	Forward Association	Backward Association
A-B, A-B	+	+	+
A-B, C-B	+	0	−
A-B, A-D	0	−	0
B-B, C-D	0	0	0

are unrelated. In this case, none of the component processes can contribute to transfer and the overall effect is zero.

The role of response meaningfulness and degree of original learning in transfer can be interpreted by means of Table 6-3 as follows. In the A-B, C-B case with low meaningful words such as nonsense syllables, the degree of first list learning determines whether there will be a positive or negative transfer effect. When material is unfamiliar, most initial learning time is spent in learning what the responses are (since responses must be produced before performance can be scored). Thus, whatever we learn about the response will carry over to the second task. For low meaningful items and low degree of first list learning, there will generally be a positive transfer in the A-B, C-B condition. On the other hand, if we allow considerable time to be spent on the first list, response learning will be complete and individuals will have time to form associations. As associations are learned, backward associations appear, which contribute negatively to overall performance. Thus, when response meaningfulness is low and degree of first list learning is high, we typically find less positive transfer than when degree of original learning is low.

It is also possible to infer from Table 6-3 that when response meaningfulness is high (for example, adjectives or nouns are used rather than nonsense syllables), only a small amount of time will be needed to learn the responses. In this case, individuals will very quickly begin to form associations. And even when degree of original learning is low, response learning can contribute very little to second task performance. We would therefore expect less positive transfer in the A-B, C-B conditions than in either of the above two cases. The A-B, C-B condition is the most complex transfer design. We can find either positive or negative transfer depending on the interaction between independent variables such as response meaningfulness and degree of original learning.

The effect of response meaningfulness and degree of first list learning on the other conditions specified in Table 6-3 is usually as follows. In A-B, A-B, whatever is learned on the first task will help on the second task, that is, as either response meaningfulness or degree of first list learning increases, positive transfer increases. In the A-B, A-D condition, the responses are different in the two tasks, so response meaningfulness is not a relevant variable. Degree of original learning makes a difference, however, since the strength of forward associations (A-B) that interfere with the acquisition of A-D are a function of first task learning. The stronger the A-B associations are, the greater is the negative transfer. Finally, in *A-B, C-D,* neither response meaningfulness nor degree of original learning can directly influence second task performances since both stimuli and responses in the second task are different from the first task.

The Use of Transfer Designs

A word of caution is in order concerning the interpretation of transfer designs. Although we typically write an analysis of two tasks with the first task being the same in all cases (see Figure 6-1 and Table 6-3), the tasks are run in the reverse order in the laboratory. We can only compare the effect of one task on another if all groups are performing the same second task (recall Tables 6-1 and 6-2).

The component analysis of transfer represented in Table 6-3 is the most powerful way to study the effect of one task on another. We use this analysis only if we have some way of describing performance such as we had in the case of the paired associates task. However, one danger of such an analysis is that once we have taken behavior apart we may not be able to put it back together again. In other words, in breaking actual behavior up into its various components, we may destroy precisely what we wish to study. This is especially true when we are concerned with skilled behavior. We can achieve fairly powerful descriptions of "pieces" of laboratory behavior, but these pieces may be unique to the laboratory and not part of the behavior displayed by the individual in practical situations.

In any event, the kind of learning that we encounter in the natural setting does not often readily lend itself to a component process analysis, and we must be satisfied with a description of transfer in terms of overall relationships between two tasks. In this case, we can fall back on an explanation for transfer effects initially formulated by Edward L. Thorndike. He suggested that transfer is found when elements of two tasks are identical with one another. The degree of transfer between two situations is then a function of the number of elements they have in common (law of identical elements).

In addition to using transfer designs to determine the effect of a first task on a second task, we employ them to determine the nature of first task acquisition. We used transfer designs in Chapter 5, for example, where we attempted to determine what concepts were learned as a result of performing in either a reception or selection learning situation. Transfer designs were used in this sense to determine what individuals have actually learned in a first task, apart from the performance that they demonstrate on that task. Recall that in order to make inferences about learning, we count responses that individuals make as either correct or incorrect and then construct graphs that represent the number of such responses as a function of time or practice. From the performance curves generated in a typical learning situation, we can gather information about the things that individuals have learned in that situation. Individuals may also learn things that are not embodied in performance as we score it. In order to determine what has been learned in addition to what was scored as correct or incorrect, we need a second task.

Let us consider an example similar to the one proposed in Chapter 5. In this case, suppose we have words printed on cards where each word is presented in a separate color. The task for the subject is to learn to associate numbers with the words (paired associates learning). After first task performance in which the subjects learn to correctly pair numbers with words on the cards, we ask whether they have learned to respond to color, to words, or to the combination of color and words. As was the case in Chapter 5, the independent variables of color and words are completely confounded and the subject can perform correctly on the first task by responding to either of these variables. To determine what subjects learned in the first task we need to give some subjects color as a stimulus on a second task and some subjects just words. In addition, of course, we should also give some subjects the combination of color and words as a control condition.

In the above situation, we refer to the stimulus that the subject learns as the functional stimulus and the stimulus that the experimenter presents as the nominal stimulus. The nominal stimulus is the one that the experimenter thinks the subject is learning (for example, colored words). The functional stimulus is the one that the subject actually learns (for example, colored words, color, or words). In most performance situations, we hope that the nominal and functional stimulus are the same and, if they are not, then we have an inadequate description of the learning that has taken place.

Nonspecific Transfer Effects

The types of transfer effects that we have considered thus far are specific. It is also possible to ask about nonspecific transfer effects. By nonspecific we mean that performance in the second task is either increased or decreased in relation to a control group and that we are unable to attribute this change to the variables being manipulated. For example, it is typically the case that if we have individuals learn a paired associates list such as we discussed in our example in Table 6-3, they will demonstrate considerable positive transfer due simply to learning how to perform in the paired associates situation (that is, performance on C-D, A-B will be greater than just A-B). To control for this possibility in assessing transfer effects, we must have individuals perform on two paired associate tasks, the first of which is different from the task given to the experimental group but the second of which is the same. Thus, A-B, C-D is a standard control for nonspecific transfer when studying, for example, A-B, C-B, because we run the groups as illustrated in Table 6-4.

Paired associates learning is not the kind of task ordinarily found in everyday experience. When individuals come into the psychologist's laboratory they must learn how to perform in the situation that the psychologist has constructed for them. We may view this kind of learning as nonspecific transfer. We generally use the terms "learning-to-learn" when nonspecific transfer is long-term and "warm-up" when it is of relatively short duration. The short-term effects must be taken into account each time we bring the subject into the laboratory even though he may be an experienced learner in the task we have set before him.

Nonspecific transfer effects can also be found in the case of animal learning where they are usually referred to as learning sets. Suppose that we give a group of monkeys the task of learning several oddity problems as illustrated in Figure 6-2. In each problem, we present an array of three stimuli to the monkey. Two of the stimuli are alike in some way and the third is different. The task for the monkey is to learn to pick out or to choose the odd stimulus, thereby gaining a reward such as a banana. Over many trials on different tasks, we find positive transfer in the sense that the monkey will learn to always pick the

TABLE 6-4
Order of Tasks in a
Typical Transfer Design

	First Task	Second Task
Group 1	C-B	A-B
Group 2		A-B
Group 3	C-D	A-B

FIGURE 6-2
Oddity problem (each row represents one task).

odd stimulus. At this point, we are tempted to say he has learned how
to do the problem. He has learned what we called in Chapter 5 a
rule.

Another example of a similar sort is illustrated in Figure 6-3. In
the first task, subjects are presented with discrimination problems consist-

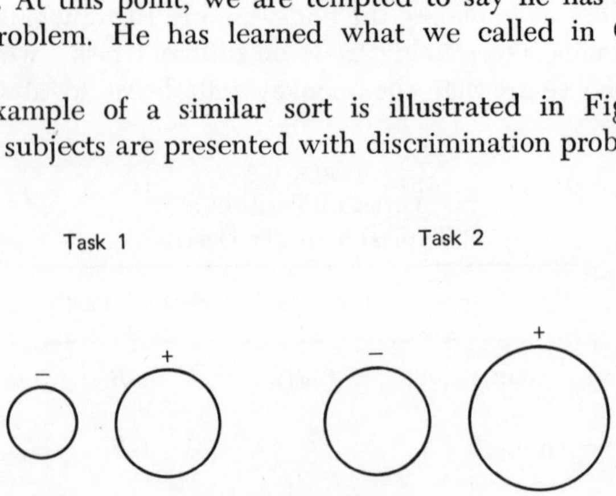

Task 1   Task 2

FIGURE 6-3
Transposition problem.

ing of two circles and they must learn to always choose the larger one. On a second task, where the smallest circle is now the same size as the larger circle in the first task, we see which circle they will choose. If, on the first task, the subjects learned to respond to particular properties of the larger circle (such as, its diameter or area) then we would expect them to choose this same circle as correct in the second task. What very often happens, however, is that, in the second task, subjects (animals as well as children) pick the larger of the two circles. This phenomenon is called transposition and refers to the ability of subjects to make relational discriminations. That is, on the first task subjects learn to respond to the relation "larger than," instead of to the larger circle per se. This learning is then transferred to the second task where the subjects continue to respond on the basis of a relationship between the stimuli.

It is worth noting that learning to learn is probably the most important kind of learning that takes place in the typical school situation. Instead of learning specific subject matter content, we hope that students will learn how to learn a subject matter—that is, that they will learn how to learn physics or learn how to learn mathematics. This idea is at the heart of the recommendation of some psychologists and curriculum builders that any subject matter can be written in some form for any child at any age. The notion is that what we are transmitting is not specific subject matter content, but the rules that govern the way the subject matter is "done."

Summary

Transfer designs are used in two ways. First, they are a means of determining whether performance on a second task can be affected by means of practice on a previous task. And second, they are a means of determining what has been learned in a given performance situation. In this latter case, we employ a second task whose independent variables are in some way related to those of the first task. In either case, we attempt to describe between-task differences in performance and the nature of these differences. To the extent that we can isolate sources that contribute to performance differences, we label them specific and manipulate them as independent variables. When sources of transfer cannot be isolated, we must describe the differences between tasks by the use of terms such as rules. The variables of nonspecific transfer are in this sense like the macroscopic variables referred to at the end of Chapter 4 and about which we shall have more to say in the final chapter.

Suffice it to say for now that the goal of instruction is to optimize transfer. In other words, what we want to achieve in most educational situations is maximum transfer between one learning situation and another. And if we want transfer we should teach for it. To do this we must keep in mind, however, that the effects we observe on learning might not necessarily be the same as those we observe on retention. It can happen, for instance, that a task that is difficult to learn may facilitate the acquisition of a second task, but nonetheless contribute to poor retention of that task. Stated another way, the effects of one task on another are not necessarily the same with regard to acquisition and retention.

Suggested Readings

Ellis, H. C. *The Transfer of Learning*. Macmillan. 1965. A paperback on the introductory level. Part two contains selected articles on the use of transfer designs in research.

Hall, J. F. *The Psychology of Learning*. J. B. Lippincott Co. 1966. A thorough introductory text primarily for the student who wants a good grounding in fundamentals. Chapters 14 and 15 provide a complete discussion of all aspects of the transfer problem.

Bilodeau, E. A. *Acquisition of Skill*. Academic Press. 1966. A book of readings by prominent investigators in the field of human learning. Chapter 5 by William Battig is on an advanced level but highly stimulating. The discussion of Battig's paper on "Facilitation and Interference" by P. W. Fox, though brief, gives a nice perspective to Battig's arguments.

Underwood, B. J. *Experimental Psychology*. Appleton-Century-Crofts. 1968. Chapter 12 is an excellent complement to the present chapter. It should be read by everyone, particularly those who feel the need for an elaboration of transfer in the case of paired associate learning.

7
Remembering

"That I can't remember," said the Hatter.
"You must remember," remarked the King, "or I'll have
you executed."

How is it that we cannot remember everything that we see or hear? Although the consequences of our failure to remember things are seldom as drastic as they were for the Hatter, it is one of the most pertinent facts of our existence that we forget much of what we have learned. The carefully organized notes we studied the night before the examination cannot be remembered the next morning. The details of an experience we were determined never to forget have gradually faded away. Even the things we know well by virtue of steady repetition such as names and telephone numbers are often briefly obscured. Why do we forget?

The average individual has a preconceived model for the forgetting process based on the idea that we forget because impressions fade with time. Just as we learn and strengthen behavior by using it, so we forget and weaken behavior by not using it. This is a model of disuse, which offers a picture of the mind in which past events are gradually obliterated due to the passage of time.

There are several factors that might immediately seem wrong with such a model. To begin with, in the process of extinction as we defined it in simple conditioning, activity is present and yet associations are weakened and forgotten. In addition, the phenomenon of spontaneous recovery is a case where disuse is accompanied by an improvement in performance. Finally, as mentioned in Chapter 1, although time is a major independent variable in any science, it is only a reference variable. A piece of metal left out in the elements does not rust because of time, but because of processes that occur in time. Time itself merely provides an opportunity for effective variables to operate.

Remembering and forgetting are alternative ways of describing the same phenomena. Remembering or retention refers to the amount of learned material that persists or remains intact, whereas forgetting refers to the amount of material that has been lost. The amount retained is always measured directly and the amount forgotten is obtained by subtraction. Since the amount retained is the direct measure, it is the one typically used in constructing performance curves such as those in Chapter 3. It is useful, however, to talk about forgetting when we are considering those conditions that tend to reduce the amount of material we remember. The term forgetting is then used to refer to the absence of previously learned material with particular reference to how certain conditions, environmental events, or activities contribute to this absence.

In the typical learning situation, learning and retention are inextricably related to one another. Performance on any given trial must reflect learning that has been retained from previous trials and the learning that takes place on that particular trial. Although the terms are overlapping in what they refer to, certain operations or conventions are often used to distinguish between them.

Learning is defined and measured as progressive improvement in performance as a result of practice. No such improvement would be possible, however, if practice did not result in cumulative retention. Similarly, it would be useless to talk about retention except in reference to a level of performance achieved during learning. The practical distinction between learning and retention stems from the different times at which performance is measured.

Measures of performance obtained during a period of acquisition, that is, while the learner is working to reach some criterion, are called learning scores. Such measures describe the rate at which associations are formed and responses are built up to adequate strength. Measures of performance obtained at varying time intervals after the end of practice are considered to be retention scores. These measures show how persistent the associations are and what the changes in response strength are after a period of disuse. This suggests that the factors underlying retention are the same as those underlying learning or, conversely, that the factors underlying forgetting are the same as those that tend to slow down the learning process.

Measures of Retention

Recall

When an individual has previously learned material, we may require him to demonstrate his retention of the material by asking him to reproduce or recall as much of it as possible. For example, if we ask an individual to remember a list of words, we may score his responses, either written or spoken, in terms of the number of items he can produce. Accurate scoring of such a procedure depends on the extent to which the learned materials can be broken down into discrete items. Lists of nonsense syllables, digits, and meaningless words offer no difficulty.

A passage of connected discourse, on the other hand, does not provide equally clear-cut units. One cannot simply use the number of words correctly recalled in this case, because many of them frequently recur in the passage. Moreover, such a scoring procedure often fails to show to what degree the learner has mastered the content of the passage. For these reasons, we usually try to divide a passage of connected discourse into ideas or thought units that are estimated to be of equal difficulty, and the final retention score is then determined by the number of such thought units correctly reproduced.

There are a variety of possibilities for administering and scoring recall tests, but the method is essentially one in which the subject is given a specific opportunity to reproduce whatever he can of previously learned materials. Tests of recall constitute a very exacting method of measuring retention since only those responses or associations that have acquired sufficient strength to be available for active reproduction can contribute to an individual's performance. Associations that are not readily available have little chance of appearing in active recall, although they may aid other types of retention performance.

We may think of the minimal strength that a response must have to be actively reproduced as the threshold of its recall. Like all active thresholds, the threshold of recall is not a fixed and stable value. It fluctuates with time. As a result, an item that is not available for active reproduction at one moment may emerge above the threshold of recall at some later time. Such oscillations of the threshold of recall frequently occur in performance on tests of retention. Thus, on successive retention tests, new items not previously recalled may appear even if the total amount retained decreases. Active recall does not ordinarily yield a maximum measure of retention. Not only must responses have acquired considerable strength in order to be actively reproduced, but whatever is available for recall is subject to appreciable change from moment to moment.

Recognition

In asking an individual to remember what he has seen or heard, we may present him with previously learned material interspersed with other material of a similar nature (for example, the common multiple-choice test). In such a situation, the subject must recognize the previously seen or heard material and discriminate it from the material he has not studied. This is often a somewhat easier task than active reproduction. An individual's recognition score in such a situation depends, however, on the degree of similarity between the items that are correct and those that have been provided as fillers. Picking out the correct response is often more difficult if the items are all highly similar than if the items are dissimilar.

Since individuals in a recognition situation are to pick out the items that they recognize as correct, such a test inevitably invites guessing. Some people are, of course, more inclined to guess than others. Nevertheless, a correction for guessing may be introduced, which makes the scores of different individuals roughly comparable. A typical correction involves subtracting the percent of items incorrectly recognized from the percent correctly recognized. For example, if the original learning material consisted of twenty words and these twenty words are mixed with forty new ones on a recognition test, an individual who recognized ten words correctly but also makes four wrong identifications would receive a recognition score of 40% [that is, $(10/20-4/40)$ 100]. Another subject, who may also have recognized ten words correctly but in addition makes twenty incorrect recognitions, would receive a score of 0. With adjustment for guessing, the same number of correct recognitions may result in widely differing retention scores.

All incorrect recognitions are not necessarily the result of random guessing, but may be due simply to poor learning so that the subject is unable to discriminate between correct and incorrect items. A penalty for wrong responses is in order, however, if a fair estimate of retention is to be made (it should be pointed out that there are a number of ways to correct for guessing and that we have chosen one of the simplest of these for purposes of illustration).

It is usually easier to recognize material than it is to actively reproduce it. This result is not surprising if we consider the differences between the two test situations. All correct items appear on the recognition test. Those items that have been learned poorly may be strengthened by the very fact of their reappearance as test stimuli. Many weakly learned items, though not mastered sufficiently for active recall, are still more easily recognized when contrasted with entirely new items. In active recall, the learner has no opportunity to be exposed once more to correct items, nor can he benefit from the differences between weakly learned items and even weaker wrong items. Much of what the learner has acquired during practice cannot manifest itself in active recall because it falls short of the threshold or minimum degree of mastery that is required for active reproduction. The recognition situation is more sensitive because weaker associations have a better opportunity to contribute to an individual's performance.

Relearning

Instead of asking an individual to actively reproduce or recognize materials that have appeared in his past experience, we may require him to relearn the material at some later time. The difference between the number of trials or opportunities required to learn the material initially and the number of trials required to relearn it is then considered to be an index of retention. This index is often referred to as a savings score.

Although frequently used as a measure of retention, the method of relearning is a confounded measure since it depends on a second learning situation, which brings into play the role of learning variables. That is, the subject necessarily relearns the task sometime after original learning. During this interval, he may have become a more practiced learner. Part of the savings score that appears during the second test of retention may therefore be due, not to retention of the original material, but to a greater learning ability.

This objection may be handled, at least in part, by comparing relearning with the learning of an equivalent new task rather than with learning of the original material. The validity of the relearning procedure then depends on our ability to construct a new task that is strictly equivalent to the original learning task. With nonsense materials, equivalent lists can usually be constructed without too much difficulty. With meaningful material, such as that found in connected discourse, the problem of obtaining equivalent tasks is considerably more difficult. The special value of the method of relearning lies in the fact that it measures retention independent of the availability of specific responses. An individual may not be able to recall or recognize a single item and yet he will show a substantial amount of savings.

Temporal Characteristics

In addition to studying retention by asking individuals to recall, to recognize, or to relearn materials to which they have been exposed in the past, we may also obtain information about the degree of retention by observing an individual's behavior during these tests. In other words, we may examine the nature as well as the results of his performance.

The temporal characteristics of responses that appear in behavior are often sensitive indices of degree of retention. Probably the most frequently used temporal characteristic is latency, that is, how soon after the presentation of test material the subject gives his responses. In most situations, we think of latency as being inversely related to associative strength—the smaller the latency the greater the degree of association between stimulus and response.

It is important to consider the nature of an individual's performance since different individuals may recall or recognize the same number of items on a test of retention, yet differ widely in the nature of their performance. Thus, two individuals who have both learned a twenty-item list might reproduce all items correctly in a test of active recall. Yet, if one individual takes two minutes to produce the twenty items whereas another individual takes twenty seconds, there is clearly a sense in which the two individuals differ as regards their retention of the materials.

Curve of Forgetting

If we look systematically at the amount of material an individual can remember as a function of time since learning, we find, with few exceptions, that the amount remembered becomes less and less as the time interval between learning and recall is lengthened. We characterize this way of looking at memory by a performance curve, which is often called the curve of forgetting. Such a curve appears in Figure 7-1.

This curve is obtained by plotting time as an independent variable and some measure of retention such as recall, recognition, or savings as the dependent variable. The most striking feature of the forgetting curve is its rapid drop. This means that most material is forgotten during the first few hours after practice. In fact, in the first few hours following practice an individual may forget as much as 40 percent of what he

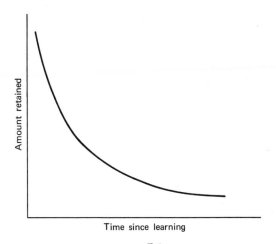

Time since learning

FIGURE 7-1

Typical "curve of forgetting" (retention curve).

has learned. After the first day, the decline is much slower and the slope of the curve of forgetting is very gradual. Although there is no truly typical forgetting curve, the initial rapid decline is a feature common to curves obtained for many different kinds of situations.

The gentle slope in the latter part of the forgetting curve suggests that forgetting very slowly, if ever, becomes complete. As we suggested earlier, a certain amount of savings can be expected even after extended periods of time. It is almost as if the effects of past learning persist indefinitely, if only our measures are sensitive enough to detect them.

Measures of retention gauge how lasting are the effects of learning. That which is strongly fixed should last longer, and, usually, the higher the degree of original learning the greater the retention. Retention cannot increase indefinitely as a function of a degree of learning, however. At some point diminishing returns are reached. Overlearning, which refers to continued practice beyond some defined level of mastery, typically yields only small increments in retention. It is worth noting, however, that extended repetition beyond mastery is only very seldom studied by the psychologist for periods of time like those involved in daily learning. Repetition beyond mastery in our everyday experience proceeds for hundreds and hundreds of trials, whereas the psychologist in his laboratory usually investigates overlearning for only ten or twenty trials.

It is important to note that not even a constant criterion of mastery, such as being able to produce all items of a list correctly twice in a row, can insure a constant degree of learning. When two different individuals satisfy this criterion, we can only conclude that at the time of testing both individuals reached some minimum degree of mastery. They may still differ in degree of learning as measured by more sensitive tests. Whether equal test performance means equal degree of learning depends, among other things, on the age of the associations involved.

This relationship (between learning, performance, and age of associations) can be derived from the forgetting in Figure 7-1. Suppose, for example, that an individual learns a list of material to a criterion on Monday. Another individual learns the material to the same criterion on Thursday. On Friday, both the first individual and the second individual show the same performance as measured by a test of retention. On a subsequent test of retention the following Monday, however, the first individual is likely to be superior to the second. This is because by Friday he has forgotten most of what he is going to forget (he is at the flat portion of his forgetting curve). The second individual, however, will forget considerable material between Friday and Monday (he is at the steeper portion of his forgetting curve).

The curve of forgetting suggests that, if two associations that meet the same criterion are of different ages, the older one will diminish less with time. In other words, the ability to reach a criterion is not an unequivocal index of the degree of learning, and whenever degree of learning is used as an independent variable we must control for the effects of using associations that are of different ages.

Since the time we allot for learning an association is an important determiner of its strength, we are generally better able to remember long tasks than short ones. A long task is more difficult to learn, of course, but when it has been learned a larger amount of time has been spent on each item than in the short task. Therefore, the associations between individual items within the long task are older and stronger than in the short one.

Another typical finding in the study of human memory is that, although individuals differ widely in the rate at which they learn a given task, once they have reached a common criterion of learning, their differences in retention will usually be small. If, for example, a slow learner and a fast learner are taken to the same level of performance, then retention for the material will, at a subsequent time, be about the same (provided, of course, that the associations are of a comparable "age"). This constancy of forgetting despite the presence of factors that make considerable differences in learning is a rather remarkable fact. It almost appears as if some factors that are quite independent of any of the variables manipulated in learning, but that are correlated with time, impose themselves on memory functioning and thereby produce the rate of loss characterized by the curve of forgetting.

Retention Variables

Because of the overlap between the concepts of learning and retention, it is of considerable importance in any discussion of remembering to distinguish between variables that affect retention per se, and variables that affect retention because they affect learning. Put another way, it is important to separate retention variables (independent variables affecting performance after acquisition) from learning variables (independent variables affecting performance during acquisition). To do this, we must construct situations in which the observation of retention is not influenced by factors that affect learning.

In general, unless some peculiar circumstances attend the situation, the greater the number of repetitions (frequency) of a given association during learning, the more resistant that association is to forgetting. The relationship between degree of learning and amount retained requires that whenever we are studying the effect of a variable other than degree of learning, we must have constant learning across all conditions. One general solution to the problem of whether something is a retention variable is to equate all subjects under consideration for degree of learning prior to the retention interval.

If it is events that take place in time that contribute to forgetting, then we must construct a framework in which we can examine the effect of such events. These events fall logically into two categories— those that take place before the material is learned and those that take place afterward. We may operationalize our thinking about these categories by constructing protypical situations for examining them as we did in the case of operant and classical conditioning in Chapter 3.

We shall use the term "retroaction" to describe the influence of subsequent events on the retention of previously learned material. And we shall use the term "proaction" to refer to the influence of previous events on the retention of subsequently learned material. These two situations are diagrammed in Figure 7-2. It is important to note that the term retroaction should not be construed to mean backward action in time. The retroaction design in Figure 7-2 implies that another learning task, interposed between learning and a test for retention of the first task, will affect our ability to remember the original material.

	Retroaction		
Group 1	Learn A	Learn B	Test on A
Group 2	Learn A		Test on A

	Proaction		
Group 1	Learn A	Learn B	Test on B
Group 2		Learn B	Test on B

FIGURE 7-2

Retroaction and proaction designs for the study of memory.

In the typical retroaction situation, we find a decrement in performance due to interference from the second task. This second task is often called interpolated learning. However, there also may be a performance decrement due to the unavailability of the original material. When we are asked to learn new associations, it may be necessary to extinguish, unlearn or set aside the previously learned material so that we can form the new associations. This is particularly true when previously learned associations are very similar to the material we must now learn. Once we unlearn associations so that we can learn new material, we may find that these associations are no longer available to us. Our performance on a test of retention for the old associations shows a decrement due not only to interference from new associations but also to the sheer unavailability of the old associations. This analysis of retroaction thus suggests two metaphors to account for forgetting, response competition and unlearning.

These metaphors can also be applied to proaction. For example, if the old and new materials are similar in some respect, then old associations will compete with the acquisition of new associations. To overcome such response competition, we extinguish the old associations. Whereas in the retroaction situation these extinguished associations are to be later recalled, in the proaction situation it is the new associations that we want to remember. Thus, unlearning or extinction does not enter directly as an explanation for forgetting. It does enter indirectly, however, in the sense that extinguished associations may reappear (that is, spontaneously recover at a later time).

In the case of retroaction, the extinguished associations are ones that contribute to correct performance on a test of retention. Any spontaneous recovery of their strength tends to decrease interference among associations on that test. In the case of proaction, however, the associations on the first list are incorrect as far as the test of retention is concerned, and the spontaneous recovery of these associations tends to increase interference.

Our analysis of performance situations into two types, retroactive and proactive, was prompted by an attempt to define retention variables. We can now see that, to be a retention variable, the variable in question must affect the strength of either the interfering associations or the correct associations at the time of recall. In the case of retroaction, the interfering associations are from the second task while in proaction they are from the first task. And, of course, the opposite is true of the correct associations in each case. Thus, retention variables include time spent learning interfering associations, time spent learning original associations (including overlearning), and time between learning tasks (allowing both for decreasing associative strength and spontaneous recovery of extinguished associations).

Improvement of Retention

Although we usually think of retention variables as being responsible for forgetting, we can also focus our attention on factors that improve our ability to remember what we see or hear. In one sense, of course, any time we manipulate variables that reduce forgetting we are automatically facilitating retention. Thus, we might attempt to reduce competition between items at the time of recall by having subjects overlearn a second list when the cause of interference is prior learning (proaction). And we may attempt to prevent the unlearning of correct responses from a first task during second task acquisition by using highly dissimilar responses in the two tasks (retroaction).

In addition to manipulating such variables, however, we can introduce variables that are less well understood, but that are considerably more effective. Examples of such variables would be mnemonic cues of one sort or another, which various individuals use to store information. For example, we might try to remember people's names by associating each person with something to eat. At the time of recall, we generate things to eat, which in turn call up the names associated with them. Such cues that are used at the time of encoding produce startling amounts of recall.

Besides cues that are employed during encoding, we can enhance retention by presenting cues at the time of recall. If, for example, we have been given a variety of words to memorize, one of which is "engineer," we might facilitate the recall of this word by being shown the word "occupation." In like manner we can "stimulate" recall by prompting individuals with words that are strongly associated with the words they are trying to remember. Thus, if we are trying to remember "woman" we might be helped by seeing the word "man."

Variables that facilitate recall and thereby reduce forgetting are only beginning to be studied systematically in the laboratory. However, such studies suggest that in assessing what an individual "knows" in any practical situation we need to take account of the full range of conditions under which he is likely to reveal the desired information.

The Memory Trace

In our discussion of retention and forgetting we have not referred to the concept of memory trace. Although an interference model of forgetting is a reasonable one when we can use the association as a unit of analysis, it is difficult to relate this model to situations in which the material to be remembered is geometric figures or connected discourse. The critical question about memory, which suggests that the association is not a sufficient unit of analysis to account for retention phenomena, is the progressive change that memory undergoes with time. In the association model, no changes are assumed to take place between points in time where performance is being produced by the organism. However, the concept of trace implies that the changes occur in memory without performance.

In the course of time, we not only remember less and less of what we have learned, but what we do remember frequently suffers transformation and distortion. We can increase our insight into the process of remembering and forgetting if we do not limit ourselves to a consideration of the sheer amount of material remembered or forgotten. We also need to consider carefully the types of qualitative changes that characterize the temporal course of memory. The twin problems of memory loss and memory change can be considered together and can be viewed as complementary aspects of the same process.

The concept of trace is embodied in the notion that memory changes occur in time quite apart from the environmental conditions and events that are imposed on the organism. In its broadest sense the term trace refers to the modification that the organism has undergone as a result of learning. Having learned, the organism is no longer the same as it was. In using the concept of trace in this way we do not necessarily imply any assumptions about the physiological or neurological correlates of learning. Trace is merely a concept that helps to extend our analysis of the memory process. It is a metaphor in the same sense as interference and is employed to describe a process inherently unavailable to study.

Our task, when we use the concept of memory trace rather than interference, is to ask how what we have learned develops and changes in time. Does our memory for past events merely deteriorate and become more and more blurred, hence, increasingly unavailable in recall, or does the memory trace change and develop in systematic ways? Let us consider some situations in which we can examine these sorts of questions in detail.

Successive Recall

One means for studying progressive change in memory over time is to present materials to individuals and to ask them to reproduce these materials at differing time intervals after original exposure. The important feature of this procedure is that the same subject is asked to reproduce the same material on several successive occasions; thus, progressive changes in reproduction can be assumed to reflect the development of the trace of the original stimulus. If we wish to study the trace in its pure form apart from the systematic distortion that the organism may impose on it in the encoding process, we need to use stimulus materials that are, in general, unfamiliar.

Both verbal and nonverbal materials are subject to distortion consistent with our past experience. One feature of our past experience that gives particular evidence of this is the verbal labels that we attach to visual materials. Such labels can drastically determine the nature of the reorganization that takes place. For example, if an individual is exposed to a highly abstract visual form that he assumes to be the picture of a cat, then regardless of whether it is a cat, when he is asked to recall this picture at some later time, he is very likely to draw what he considers to be a cat. His recall at a later time is determined by the verbal label that he has assigned to the form. Individuals often rely heavily on such responses in problem solving and learning situations in order to make sense out of otherwise unorganized materials.

Although the active recall of a single individual can give us information about the nature of the distortion and change that takes place in a memory trace, the successive reproduction of material by the same individual is subject to certain methodological criticisms. First, an individual's reproduction cannot simply be regarded as an index of the state of a trace. In reproducing a geometric design, for example, an individual is limited by performance factors such as drawing ability. A more serious difficulty, however, stems from the fact that the very act of reproduction may itself change the nature of the trace. Thus, in making successive reproductions, an individual is influenced not only by his original perception and the trace formed by it, but also by his preceding recalls. If he makes an error or introduces a distortion in the first series of recalls, he may remember his error when he attempts his second reproduction. We cannot observe the memory trace without letting it act, but in activating it we need to avoid distorting and altering its subsequent history.

Single Recall

To avoid the criticism of looking at successive recalls from a single individual, we can construct another situation in which we select several different individuals or groups of individuals, each of which is asked to recall the same material at different time intervals after the original learning. An important aspect of this procedure is that the individuals producing the recalls at different points in time have all been exposed to the original material in the same fashion and can therefore all be regarded as the same individual with respect to that material.

The pictures of forgetting yielded by the procedures of single and successive recalls are not always the same. For example, the procedures often result in different amounts of forgetting. The method of single recall typically shows a steady, increasing forgetting, which is typical of the curve in Figure 7-1. With the procedure of successive recalls, however, the changes in time are much slower. In this case, each successive reproduction is a rehearsal that serves to fixate and perpetuate what has been originally retained.

There are also qualitative differences in results obtained by the two procedures. Whereas successive recalls often yield progressive changes in time, single recalls simply become less and less accurate as the interval between original learning and retention is lengthened. The different pictures of forgetting that we obtained by using these different methods point out the dilemma we face when we attempt to chart the temporal development of an unobservable psychological process. In successive recalls by the same subject, each test is profoundly influenced by the preceding test. Recalls by different individuals at different time intervals alleviate this difficulty, but they do not yield information about the temporal development of any one single system of memory traces.

Serial Recall

The omissions, changes, and distortions that characterize the successive recalls by a single individual are exaggerated and accelerated in the procedure for studying memory, often described as serial reproduction. Here only one individual is exposed to the stimulus material. This "eyewitness" then passes on what he remembers to a second individual who in turn transmits it to a third, and so on, until the chain of reproduction has been completed. This "parlor game" type of situation has the advantage that it retains the distortions appearing in successive recalls by a single individual. On the other hand, since no one individual recalls the material more than once, the actual act of recall cannot systematically distort the trace. The initial stimulus material can be a prose passage, a picture, or anything else that exceeds our immediate memory span. In order to demonstrate this phenomenon it is usually wise to employ materials that are rather rich in detail and that are abstract enough to provide an opportunity for various types of memory change to unfold in the course of serial transmission.

In serial recall the speed and magnitude of memory distortions are at a maximum. Each successive subject in the series has nothing to rely on except the report of another individual. His retention is not anchored to any stable points of reference, and the individual who is merely a link in the chain has no general idea of the nature or content of the original material.

There is, of course, no foolproof method for studying the temporal development of an individual's memory for what he has seen or heard. Nevertheless, the types of progressive change obtained under various methods of reproduction are worth studying because of the light that they can shed on the kinds of memory functions with which we have to deal when we attempt to describe the acquisition and retention of highly complex materials. In school learning, for example, the distortions that we describe in the procedures of successive recall may well index actual processes by which individuals reproduce and scan materials for themselves when they attempt to reconstruct problem-solving situations.

Even though each successive reproduction is influenced by the preceding one, this may be exactly what happens when individuals are called on to utilize their memory in practical situations. If we want to recall a childhood experience, we cannot tap the pure trace of that experience but must recall it after it has been affected by all our previous reproductions of it. In solving an algebraic or physical equation, we are influenced by the previous times we have recalled this equation and the system of events surrounding it. Thus, even though the psychologist often tries to describe memory in a relatively pure fashion, such a description is only one kind of picture that we need in order to fully understand the memory process.

Summary

The process of memory is begun by our initial perception of a stimulus situation. Perception is selective, however, and out of the total array of stimuli only a limited portion are actually encoded. Furthermore, only those events that are favored by such perception are well retained. Not only is perception selective, but it also entails some sort of active organization and interpretation, often with the aid of verbal labels. In other words, our memory of past events and experiences and our learned habits of seeing and responding are all incorporated into a scheme or a framework that influences perception. Moreover, under the direction and influence of this scheme, our memory is continually changing.

Memory is a constructive, creative process, which actively unfolds from the very first moment of initial perception to the final act of recall. No metaphor could be less appropriate for memory than an image on a photographic plate that ultimately fades away. Whenever we recreate our past experience, we are subject to all the errors and transformations that we have accumulated since we first perceived the event that we are trying to remember.

It should be evident by now that, although we have used the term memory in a variety of ways in this chapter, we have by no means exhausted its uses. Indeed, it is one of the most general ways we have of talking about behavior. For example, we use the term to refer to the capacity for remembrance, such as our capacity for remembering to carry out duties or other observations at an appropriate time. And we use the term to refer to the amount that we can remember of past experiences, such as happy childhood memories. Our everyday use of the term memory is usually in relation to conscious experiences, but it is sometimes extended to include the capacity to retain learned verbal and motor skills such as reading, writing, and driving a car.

Memory can also be regarded as a property of living organisms that helps them to adapt to the conditions of their environment. Thus, we may think of memory as a capacity for an organism to behave in a way that is modified by previous experience. In this sense, memory includes the capacity for conditioning and delayed responding. When the term genetic memory is used, we mean, in a figurative sense, the total store of information contained in the apparatus of a living cell.

Such information enables the organism to develop characteristics of its predecessors and thereby to recapitulate the genetic history of the species. Thus, in the collective sense, memory refers to species' specific patterns of behavior such as mating, nest building, and migration, all of which are inherited by the members of a genetic strain.

The difference between the way in which we use the term memory in our daily experience and the way in which the psychologist uses the term, lies in the generality implied by the latter. The psychologist wants to understand the reasons why our memory for events changes in time, while the average individual is satisfied with a description of how these changes occur so that he can anticipate and take account of them in his own behavior.

In using the psychologist's terminology we must avoid mistaking his procedures (which serve to operationalize metaphors) with what he is attempting to explain. For by treating procedures as processes, we come to speak as if our metaphors were true. Thus, we may believe that interference is a psychological process and we may fail to remember that it is nothing more than a way of accounting for certain facts of retention and forgetting. This same criticism applies, of course, to our own preconceived metaphors. It is in the nature of human experience to attempt to describe reality in terms of familiar things. However, we must constantly be aware of the fact that whatever metaphors we employ are in no sense necessarily true of either psychological or physical experience.

Suggested Readings

Bartlett, F. C. *Remembering.* Cambridge University Press. 1961. This is the work to go to if the concept of memory trace intrigues you. Bartlett's "Egyptian Owl" experiment is a standard illustration in most introductory psychology books. The book was originally written in 1932 but has proven to be remarkably useful to the modern investigator.

Bilodeau, E. A. *Acquisition of Skill.* Academic Press. 1966. Chapter 7 on retention by Bilodeau is an excellent discussion of some new ideas in the study of memory with particular significance for the field of education. Once again, the discussion is fairly technical but well worth the extra effort. Bahrick's discussion of the Bilodeau paper should also be read.

Hall, J. F. *The Psychology of Learning.* J. B. Lippincott Co. 1966. Chapters 16 and 17 provide a thorough discussion of research findings as well as concepts. A more difficult book than Jung.

John, E. Roy. *Mechanisms of Memory.* Academic Press. 1967. For the physiologically minded. The book is highly technical and most will not want to go beyond Chapter 1, which lays out the basic issues.

Jung, J. *Verbal Learning*. Holt, Rinehart and Winston. 1968. A basic introductory text. Chapters 6 and 7 provide a discussion of modern concepts in the study of memory.

Munsat, S. *The Concept of Memory*. Random House. 1966. A critique of the concept of memory by a philosopher. The book is a paperback and deserves to be read in its entirety. Chapter 1 is sufficient for those unfamiliar with philosophical thickets.

Underwood, B. J. *Experimental Psychology*. Appleton-Century Crofts. 1966. Simpler than Hall but more complete than Jung. Chapter 13 emphasizes methodology in the study of memory. As always, Underwood is well worth reading.

Woodworth, R. S. & Schlosberg, H. *Experimental Psychology*. Holt, Rinehart and Winston. 1964. A classic text. Although some commentaries are now out of date, chapters 23 and 24 provide a useful discussion of the interrelationships between the concepts of transfer and retention.

8

Language and the Acquisition of Knowledge

"Speak English!" Said the Eaglet. "I don't know the meaning of half those long words, and, what's more, I don't believe you do either!"

Language is central to the task of schooling not only because we presumably teach individuals how to use it effectively, but also because it is the prime means in our society for storing and transmitting knowledge. In this latter sense, academic disciplines often create languages that have their own system of meaning and syntax. Although these languages sometimes contain new words, they also draw on words used in everyday discourse. Thus, we find that Newton used words such as force, mass, velocity, and attraction in formulating the theories found in his book, *Principles of Mechanics*. When familiar words are used in a subject matter, they are often given particular meanings that are new and highly restricted in scope, and as we attempt to learn these new meanings we must cope with old associations carried over from past experience.

Not only can language be viewed as a vehicle for storing and transmitting knowledge, it can also be regarded as a shaper of knowledge. Our thoughts, in this sense, are a function of the language that we use to communicate them as well as of the particular ideas that we are attempting to present. The proposed relation between language and thought can be generalized to different language systems (cultures). A linguist, Benjamin Lee Whorf, proposed, for example, that our thought patterns are shaped by the verbal environment in which we are raised.

He suggested that the Hopi Indians might have different perceptions than we do because their language contains no explicit word for the concept of time. A similar example can be constructed for the concept of snow. Although young boys may distinguish between "good packing snow" and "poor packing snow," most of us are content to use the single word "snow." Eskimos, on the other hand, often have names for as many as 27 different kinds of snow.

Presumably, individuals make discriminations among things in their environment for some reason (for example, they have survival value). However, evidence that a particular group of individuals does not make a discrimination should not be construed to mean that they cannot if we make it important and possible for them to do so. To take our previous example, even though we do not have names for many different kinds of snow, given a discrimination task such as those in Chapter 3, we may very well be able to detect the differences on which the Eskimo makes his discrimination.

As far as we are concerned, however, the point is that language can influence thought and, if academic disciplines are indeed specialized language systems, then they are shapers of thought as well as storehouses of ideas. Perhaps this is what C. P. Snow had in mind when he referred to two cultures—the arts and the sciences—and the lack of communication between them. Artists develop a language which they use to communicate with one another and so do scientists, but there is little apparent discourse between them.

Some Characteristics of Verbal Behavior

One of the simplest ways of empirically determining characteristics of verbal behavior is to count units in some defined population of discourse. We might choose, for example, to count the number of times that various words occur in a textbook on biology or history. Not only can we tabulate the frequency of occurrence of individual words, but we can also count the frequency of co-occurrence of pairs of words within units such as sentences, paragraphs, or phrases. Elaborate analyses of this kind have been done for a variety of samples of language.

The most outstanding finding from a frequency analysis of language is that there exists a relationship between the frequency of occurrence of a linguistic event, such as a word, and the number of different events that occur with this frequency. This relationship is illustrated in Figure 8-1.

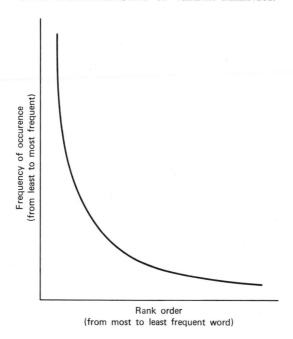

FIGURE 8-1

A standard curve of English words.

The figure shows that a few words occur often in most discourse and many words occur seldom. This is a strikingly uniform finding for many samples of different kinds of discourse. Figure 8-1 is often referred to as Zipf's law and it is commonly expressed by plotting points on axes that are logarithms. In this case, the graph is a straight line sloping down from left to right. It should be mentioned that the fact that the relation in Figure 8-1 decreases as we move from left to right on the horizontal axis is not surprising. What is of interest is the fact that for a wide variety of language samples the form of the relationship (that is, shape of the curve) is the same.

An alternative way to describe Figure 8-1 is to say that there is a relationship between the frequency of occurrence of a word and its rank, when words are ordered with respect to their frequency of occurrence in a sample of discourse. This means that a few key words do a good deal of work in communicating ideas through verbal discourse, and it is these words and their relationship with one another that an individual must learn in order to understand the ideas embodied in that discourse.

Another significant finding about our verbal behavior is that we can remember nonsense material that conforms to the rules of grammar better than we can remember nonsense material that is without any syntactic constraint. Lewis Carroll capitalized on this aspect of verbal behavior when he wrote

> "Twas brillig and the slithy toves
> Did gyre and gimble in the wabe . . ."

A similar example is the sentence, "Colorless green ideas sleep furiously." It is apparently as easy for us to remember nonsense that is grammatically correct as it is for us to remember meaningful prose. As we violate more and more rules of grammar, however, our memory for what we have just seen or heard becomes less and less accurate. The significant distinction does not seem to be between meaning and nonsense, but rather between materials that utilize previous learning and thus permit positive transfer and those materials that do not. If nonsense materials preserve associations of the English language then they are easy to learn and remember. This suggests that meaningful material is easy to learn not because it is meaningful per se but because it preserves things that are familiar to us.

Although nonsense material that conforms to the rules of grammar is easily learned and remembered, we ordinarily are interested in describing the characteristics of verbal material used to communicate meaning. The meaning of a given word can be defined in various ways. For example, it can be defined empirically by responses elicited on a word association test (for example, the meaning of "man" is woman; boy, strong). The meaning of a word can also be defined as a profile on a rating scale where the anchors of this scale are bipolar adjectives (that is, opposites such as strong-weak, good-bad). However, the empirical definition of meaning in terms of performance on such instruments has been of limited value in predicting verbal behavior. In general, we have been able to successfully predict only those kinds of verbal behavior found in highly restricted laboratory situations. When it comes to predicting language behavior such as we find in paraphrasing and everyday discourse, we find that we have not yet developed adequate variables to formulate situations for experimental study.

The Structure of Language

It is a rather remarkable fact of language that young children are capable of producing a bewildering variety of combinations of words, combinations that could not possibly have been learned. Recent thinking in psychology and linguistics has interpreted this to mean that language can be understood on multiple levels. There is, first, the surface level where we find words occurring in relation to one another with various frequencies. Surface structure can be indexed empirically as described earlier in terms of the frequency of occurrence and co-occurrence of individual linguistic units. Although language has surface structure, it can also be described at "deeper" levels. Here we are concerned with the rules that can be written to produce surface regularities (word patterns) and the systems of rules that can be used to describe the way in which these regularities are related to one another.

One way of making the distinction between the levels of language is to refer to the deeper level as competence and the surface level as performance. And it is the rules at the deeper level that describe, in some sense, what the child knows when he is able to use language proficiently. In using rules of competence to talk about what the speakers of a language "know," we must keep in mind that such rules are typically constructed by the linguist to describe ideal verbal behavior. In other words, these rules serve to establish the criteria for acceptable language behavior but they do not by themselves produce the strings of words found in the verbal behavior of any particular individual. To accomplish this, we need a model for verbal performance—one that will tell us how an individual produces the regularities among words that we find are characteristic of his verbal behavior.

Communication and Instruction

Very simply, we can characterize communication as a discriminative response made by an organism to some stimulus situation. But communication in teaching and in our everyday experience is broader than this. Communication has a social function; it is used to transmit ideas. Moreover, it is governed, we suppose, by some describable set of rules. Communication is, in other words, a means of sharing aspects of our experience according to a set of rules.

For communication to take place, we must first establish a lexicon or set of symbols that have agreed upon meanings. Once a group of individuals has adopted a set of symbols and rules for combining them, we must obey the rules if we wish to communicate with members of the group. Thus, if everyone agrees to call an animal with four legs, a tail, and a very long neck, a giraffe, we can no longer call such animals by other names. Likewise, within the language systems that define particular subject matter knowledge, once we specify how force, or culture, or pleistocene are to be used, we are no longer free to use those words in arbitrary ways.

Communication is a special and important kind of behavior that has the function of transmitting messages from one individual to another. We can conceptualize communication by supposing that every message has a source and a destination, and that, in order for the message to travel between its source and destination, there must be a means of transmission. Information and ideas must also be placed in appropriate forms for transmission. The operation of transforming information for transmission is called encoding. The receiver or individual on the other end of the communication system then converts the encoded messages into meanings through an operation referred to as decoding. We usually think of codes in terms of particular highly specialized symbol systems, but any language system can conform to this terminology. Thus, the French language is one sort of code and the German language is another. And subject matters such as history or geology are also codes.

Instruction can be understood as the use of language to communicate concepts, skills, and attitudes in some domain of knowledge. This language (which we shall call a subject matter language) is a code; it is characterized by technical words, special usages for common words, and syntactic and stylistic restrictions that eliminate ambiguity. In some cases, such as mathematics, this code appears almost exclusively in writing due to the fact that there are no vocal equivalents for many of its elements. A reasonable goal for the psychological analysis of instruction is a description of the independent variables of subject matter language and the manner in which these variables are related to measures of learning and understanding.

Linguistic Variables

One source of hypotheses about the variables of instruction is the description of language provided by the linguist. We cannot afford to ignore the manner in which certain parts of speech or types of sentences in a message are related to the comprehension of its content. On the other hand, it is reasonable to suppose that variables such as these are not truly at the heart of instruction, which is constructed after all for communication rather than linguistic reasons. Although linguistic variables are relevant to an understanding of instruction, they are variables that must be controlled when we want to examine the knowledge that the instruction was formulated to communicate.

The psychological problem posed by communication that employs a subject matter language is essentially one of semantics rather than syntax. However, the linguist has not achieved an understanding of meaning comparable to his understanding of syntax. Although we must recognize the role that linguistic variables play in communication, we can learn most about the use of language in school learning by focusing first on the extralinguistic variables of subject matter language and second, on the manner in which these variables are related to measures of acquisition.

Subject Matter Variables

To describe the extralinguistic variables of any subject matter language we must first distinguish between instruction that is formulated to communicate the articulated content of a discipline (what is known), and instruction that attempts to communicate the unspecified art of producing or creating that content. Although instruction in the first sense has been successful in a wide variety of contexts, instruction in the second sense has been successful almost exclusively in the personal contact of master and apprentice. We shall base our analysis of instructional variables on communication of the first kind, that is, the content of a discipline as it is written down in textbooks, monographs, and journals.

To understand the role of subject matter variables in communication, these variables must be described. However, at present, we have no well-formulated description of subject matter language. The corpus of material from which a description of subject matter variables could be derived are the materials used to communicate the content of the field. An additional corpus is the writings of specialists when they characterize or "talk about" their discipline. Even here, however, the variables are seldom explicitly stated and must be inferred from intuition and content analysis.

An empirical analysis of discourse in an area of knowledge presumes some unit of analysis. We might, for example, do a frequency count of key words or symbols. Apart from key words and symbols, initial possibilities for units of analysis are various kinds of word groupings. Although it is possible to use a linguistic unit such as the sentence in establishing these groupings (for example, counting the words that co-occur with a given word within sentences) it is more likely to be fruitful to base our empirical analysis on "natural units" in the subject matter (such as equations, definitions, metaphors, and analogies). It is well to remember that the structure of a subject matter may itself impose constraints on a description of the language by which it is communicated.

Once we have some description of the basic units employed in the communication of a subject matter, we can ask informants (for example, physicists, historians, and teachers) to sort and arrange these units so as to achieve ideas about order and structure. The structure imposed by informants as well as the frequency characteristics determined by empirical analysis defines a population of interrelated "content words." These words, together with the rules that relate them to one another, provide a first approximation to a description of subject matter variables. Once we have such a description for an area of knowledge we can ask about the sense in which its elements function as independent variables in acquisition.

Dependent Variables

To describe instruction in a given subject matter language, we need some idea about the dependent measures that define what it means to learn and understand that language. An informant is once again a useful source of information. That is, one source of hypotheses about the extralinguistic knowledge required for an interpretation of instruction is the judgment of individuals who are competent in the subject matter. A description of knowledge in this sense, as noted in Chapter 5, usually takes the form of behaviors and abilities that are implied by the instruction. These are determined by answers to the question, "What should a person be able to do who knows X", where X is some portion of the subject matter being taught.

The behavioral framework used to define knowledge in the above sense can be filled out, so to speak, by sampling from a population of informants and by writing rules that generate the behaviors supplied by them. Such performance rules may also specify behaviors not supplied by informants. Although some of these behaviors may not be accepted by informants as representing the concepts under consideration, they should be included in the behaviors that define a knowledge of these concepts. We must keep in mind that an informant may be unable to describe completely how his subject matter is done, much as the native speaker of a language is unable to articulate the grammar that furnishes a description of his utterances in that language.

The behaviors that the informant uses to represent knowledge often ıke the form of problem solving and discrimination tasks and usually, 'though not always, they involve certain skills of subject matter expresion (for example, logical or mathematical arguments). In addition, tasks f this sort, which we shall call veridical tasks, can generally be scored orrect or incorrect on the basis of subject matter rules, that is, content. hese tasks are useful measures of acquisition to the extent that they present what the individuals have learned from instruction. If, however, the tasks do not represent what individuals have learned, we have ained little information except that they cannot be done successfully.

Tasks that do not have the above-mentioned properties, that do not resume the skills of subject matter expression, and cannot logically e scored correct or incorrect by means of subject matter content, we ıall call nonveridical tasks (for example, paired associates learning, ee recall, word association, ratings of similarity among concepts, and rouping words together). These tasks specify behavioral correlates of ontent and they index acquisition not necessarily found in performance n veridical tasks. A more general rationale for using nonveridical tasks that they allow us to describe the psychological processes underlying ehavior.

Experimentation

Given some understanding of the extralinguistic variables of subject ıatter language, it is reasonable to ask how we can describe the role ıey play in the acquisition of instruction. That is, we want to know ow subject matter variables are related to dependent measures such problem-solving tests and essay tests. Our analysis of subject matter nd the instruction formulated to communicate it is in terms of stimulus nd task variables. We must keep in mind, however, that ultimately elationships between independent and dependent variables must be escribed against a background level of competence (that is, any complete description of subject matter language and the instruction that mbodies it must eventually deal with the learner himself).

Although subject matter variables can be used to generate the basic ontent of instruction, they are not necessarily psychological variables. ubject matter variables are useful in studying instruction in two reects. First, they are a source of hypotheses about the independent ariables (nominal stimuli) of the language used to communicate conepts. Subject matter variables represent psychological variables (funconal stimuli) to the extent that they account for discrimination and eneralization among concepts in appropriate tasks. The second sense

in which subject matter variables are useful is as a source of stimulu
materials which can be used with informants to determine depende
variables (that is, to obtain a behavioral description of what it mea
to know a subject matter).

One of our first problems in testing subject matter variables to se
whether they are psychological variables is sampling. Although we us
ally give considerable attention to sampling subjects, we often forg
to sample stimulus materials and dependent measures. In many case
particularly when we are concerned with language, it is as importa
to be able to generalize to populations of words or other units of analysi
and to measures of acquisition and understanding, as it is to generali
to a population of individuals whose behavior is being described (reca
Chapter 2).

To adequately sample stimulus materials, we must have a well-define
domain of content. The traditional difficulty has been in specifying som
reasonably "natural" domain of subject matter. We could, of cours
define a restricted population of materials and then choose individua
for whom this material is appropriate. For example, in the descriptic
of language we could limit ourselves to a group of two or three hundre
words and study young children. It is also possible to construct "art
ficial" content (for example, a nonsense science) whose characteristi
can be specified with considerable confidence. Although it is difficu
to be sure exactly what research on communication of such conte
tells us about the psychological characteristics of a more natural subje
matter, it does allow us to utilize directly experimental skills and tec
niques from the laboratory.

In the case of subject matter language, the words abstracted fro
an analysis of samples of communication provide an initial set of mat
rials for generating instructional materials. As far as dependent measur
are concerned, the behaviors arrived at by presenting these words
informants provide a reasonably representative index of what it mea
to know the subject matter veridically, depending, of course, on tl
characteristics of the sample of informants (that is, it is not unreasonab.
for there to be a lack of commonality among the tasks suggested l
informants to test for the acquisition of a subject matter).

Tasks such as word association, recognition, recall, paired associat
learning, and rating scales can be employed together with transfer d
signs to determine what individuals have learned. In this case, our go
is usually to specify changes in performance as a function of stage
acquisition. However, nonveridical tasks may also be used with info

ants in order to identify the overlap in performance between the
arner and the informant.

Summary

The study of any discipline begins by mapping the domain of knowl-
ge represented by its language. Independent variables obtained from
ch mappings can then be related to the behaviors that define a knowl-
ge of the discipline, both after exposure to instruction in the laboratory
tting as well as under conditions of more sustained exposure, such as
ose that occur in the classroom.

In one sense, the experiments that describe the relationship between
e independent and dependent variables of instruction are like tradi-
onal psychological experiments. In another sense, however, they are
ite different. In the study of instruction, we cannot afford to be con-
rned simply with a description of the relationship between categories
dependent and independent variables. By its very nature, instruction
mands that we concern ourselves with optimizing known relationships
tween variables. And it is the problem of optimization that is at the
art of school learning.

Optimization experiments are usually characterized by their focus on
e selection and sequencing of stimulus material. Decisions about selec-
n and sequencing are typically made to achieve criteria such as the
ortest possible acquisition time, the widest possible range of general-
ation of veridical behavior, the fewest number of errors, or some
mbination of these criteria. In constructing sequences of material for
struction, we should take account of the role of linguistic variables
comprehension. In other words, before manipulating content or se-
ence variables in a subject matter language, we want to be certain
at comprehension has been achieved as far as the linguistic variables
this language are concerned (for example, is the discourse stated
clearly and simply as possible). Research findings on the nature of
ridical behaviors (such as problem solving) may also be useful in
nerating sequencing hypotheses when the performance being opti-
ized is complex.

Major sources for generating hypotheses about the sequencing of sub-
ct matter material are the individual teacher and subject matter special-
. However, the decisions that an informant makes about how content
ould be arranged for purposes of instruction will very likely be differ-
t from the decisions that he makes in describing the content in the

first place. Moreover, given agreement as to the content to be communi
cated, there may be considerable variation among informants as to ho
it should be sequenced. Thus, it is important that we once again mak
the specialist or teacher a sampling variable. Of course, we can alway
use ourselves as informants both in describing content and in makir
decisions about its sequencing. But unless we have a good knowledg
of the subject matter being communicated, our own intuition is n
likely to be fruitful except in highly specific situations.

Suggested Readings

Arnheim, R. *Toward A Psychology of Art.* Univ. of Calif. Press. 1966.
    book of essays that effectively bridges the gap between theory an
    practice. Chapters 1 and 6 are particularly valuable for the teach
    The introduction by Ernest Nagel is excellent.
Ausubel, D. *The Psychology of Meaningful Verbal Learning.* Grune and Stra
    ton. 1963. An extraordinarily difficult book to read, partly because
    the dense prose and partly because Ausubel has a tendency to use ne
    words where old ones would do. Chapter 7 is a nice critique of t
    discovery process in knowledge acquisition.
Bellack, A. et al. *The Language of the Classroom.* Teachers College Pre
    1966. Another research monograph. Chapter 1 is a useful discussi
    of the role of language in school learning. Chapter 9 is an interesti
    description of the "game" of school.
Brown, Roger. *Words and Things.* Free Press. 1958. A highly readable accou
    of a number of significant topics by an outstanding psychologist. T
    introduction is directly relevant to this chapter. Chapters 2–7 give
    extremely informative account of such things as reading, linguistic va
    ables, and meaning.
Cherry, Colin. *On Human Communication.* The MIT Press. 1966. A clas
    book. The approach is scholarly and it is extremely well written. Chapte
    1–3 and 7 are probably the most valuable for the moderately interest
    reader.
Church, J. *Language and the Discovery of Reality.* Random House. 196
    Some of the major issues and problems relating language and thoug
    are described in Chapters 5 and 6. Chapter 7 is a good discussion
    assessment techniques.
Deese, J. *The Structure of Associations in Language and Thought.* Jo
    Hopkins Press. 1965. A research monograph. Chapters 1 and 8 provi
    a contrast of the classic and modern associationist views on the re
    tionship between language and thought.
Dixon, T. R., & Horton, D. L. (Eds.) *Verbal Behavior and General Behav*

Theory. Prentice-Hall, Inc. 1968. A book of contributed papers. Most presentations are quite technical and presume considerable background. The book is included here largely to provide readings on the emerging field of psycholinguistics. These can be found in Chapters 15–19. Chapters 20–21, which attempt to summarize the rest of the book, are well written and also worth reading.

Elam, S. (Ed.) *Education and the Structure of Knowledge.* Rand McNally and Co. 1964. Another book of collected papers. Chapters 1, 5, and 8 provide a good overview of the general problem of defining a structure of knowledge.

Ford, G. W., & Pugno, L. (Eds.) *The Structure of Knowledge and the Curriculum.* Rand McNally. 1964. A short book of essays, each devoted to a different discipline. The introductory essay by Schwab is probably the most valuable.

Gerbner, G. et al. (Eds.) *The Analysis of Communication Content.* John Wiley and Sons, 1969. Contributed papers on techniques and theories of content analysis. These are the tools of the trade, so to speak, for those who might wish to describe the "subject matter variables" in some area of knowledge.

Miller, George. *Language and Communication.* McGraw-Hill Company, Inc. 1951. A classic text. The whole book is worth reading. For the mildly interested reader, Chapters 1, 4, and 7–11 are probably sufficient.

Osgood, C., Suci, G. & Tannenbaum, P. *The Measurement of Meaning.* University of Illinois Press. 1964. A psychological monograph on research and theory surrounding a particular technique for assessing meaning. The theory is contained in Chapter 1, the technique in Chapter 3.

Pearson, Karl. *The Grammar of Science.* Meridan Books, Inc. 1957. A timeless perspective on the nature of a discipline. Although out of date as regards the content of modern science, the procedures of analysis are still valid.

Pierce, J. R. *Symbols, Signals and Noise.* Harper and Row. Inc. 1961. A simple, clearly written introduction to communication theory. Chapters 1, 6, 8, and 9 are useful for the general reader.

Scheffler, I. *Conditions of Knowledge.* Scott, Foresman and Co. 1965. By a philosopher. The book is an invaluable guide to the uses and misuses of terminology, particularly for the practitioner. It should be on the reading list of every teacher.

White, M. *Foundations of Historical Knowledge.* Harper and Row, 1965. An example of a statement as to what a discipline "is." It is this kind of writing that must be utilized if we are to properly describe knowledge.

Whorf, B. L. *Language, Thought and Reality.* The MIT Press. 1956. The classic statement of linguistic relativity. The book consists of selected papers. The introduction by John Carroll provides a good perspective on Whorf's work.

9

Toward a Psychology of School Learning

"Would you tell me, please, which way I ought to go from here?" (asked Alice).
"That depends a good deal on where you want to get to," said the Cat.

We have described some major phenomena of learning as they are studied and understood by the science of psychology. But more than this, we have attempted to construct a framework for describing school learning behavior that will facilitate teaching, counseling, and curriculum decisions.

Our framework is based on the assumption that school learning is a complex process, many components of which are highly specific kinds of human behavior. Such was the case, for example, when we discussed behavior modification in Chapter 4 based on models formulated to describe conditioned responses. Here we viewed teaching, in part, as a process of establishing behavioral control over the individuals who are attempting to learn. That this control can be described by models that are constructed for animal behavior does not detract from their usefulness.

We also used models for human rote learning to describe conceptual behavior and the way in which learned behavior is transferred and remembered. Once again, we assumed that aspects of school learning can be understood by means of models that are constructed to describe relatively specialized kinds of behaviors. At the same time that we use such models to interpret school learning, we must realize that the class-

110

room is a unique behavioral system that demands description in its own right. Such a description is the subject of this final chapter.

Systems Analysis

The models for learned behavior that we have considered thus far are based on a view of the organism as a "black box." We have supposed that information is put into the box; we characterize this information by the term stimulus. By virtue of its internal mechanisms, the box operates on the information and transforms or changes it. This transformed information appears as output, which we characterize as a response (see Figure 9-1). The science of psychology attempts to describe relationships between stimuli and responses, and models are constructed to account for the observed regularities between them.

When we predict behavior of others by means of informal or prescientific experience, we also depend on correlations between various kinds of input and behavior. In this case, however, we usually do not construct explicit models to account for the regularities we observe. Instead, we base our predictions on what we have learned about the behavior of individuals around us (that is, we construct an informal model or metaphor).

The "black box" model for behavior is limited in the sense that what we typically describe is the behavior if a single, idealized organism and school learning characteristically involves many individuals learning simultaneously in a variety of ways. To take account of some of the complexities of the classroom situation, we construct the framework in Figure 9-2.

Figure 9-2 represents a behavioral system consisting of several components. These components might include learner variables such as socioeconomic background, language habits, age, sex, and learning ability and also teacher variables such as teaching style, age, sex, and subject matter competence. To understand the relationships illustrated in this figure, we must change our thinking about the functional description

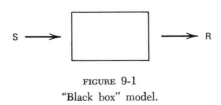

FIGURE 9-1
"Black box" model.

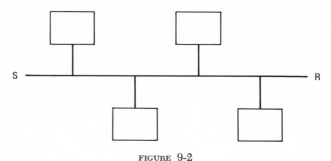

FIGURE 9-2
Modified "black box" model for behavioral systems.

of behavior proposed in Chapter 2. Recall that this description had the form $R = F(S)$ where R represents a response made by an individual to a stimulus, S. The basic problem in this framework is to find a functional relationship that best describes the responses individuals make under specific, well-defined conditions. In Figure 9-2, however, we have several functional relationships represented by the various boxes, and our task is to describe the relationship between responses and stimuli as a function of what we shall call macroscopic variables and collective parameters.

Macroscopic variables are one class of independent variables that can be used to define the state of a system. As we pointed out at the end of Chapter 4, these variables represent "observable" characteristics of some phenomenon. To take an example from physics, position and velocity are macroscopic variables when we are describing an actual falling body, but they are microscopic variables when we are describing the state of a gas (composed of hypothetical particles). Whether a given set of variables is macroscopic or microscopic depends on how we view a phenomenon and the level of explanation we want to achieve.

To complete our description of a behavioral system in the sense of Figure 9-2, we must state whether its macroscopic variables change with time. If they do, the system is a dynamic one. On the other hand, if the macroscopic variables in a system do not depend on time, we say the system is static.

In addition to variables, systems have parameters. The idea of a parameter is widely used in stating functional relationships. For example, we may write the general description of a straight line as $y = mx + b$. The m and b in this equation are parameters and the x and y are variables, y being the dependent variable and x being the independent variable.

The functional relationship $y = mx + b$ actually specifies a whole family or collection of straight lines. Specific values that are given to m and b identify some particular line from this collection.

In the same way, parameters specify particular values that apply to a given behavioral system. When these parameters refer to macroscopic variables, as they do in the present case, we call them collective parameters. Notice, however, that because we specify values for the parameters of a system does not mean it is constant in time. In other words, by specifying a particular set of parameter values, we define a system. Whether the system is a static or dynamic system depends on its variables.

Of course, before we can begin to determine values for the parameters of a system, we need to have a description of the relationship between the independent and dependent variables of that system. As illustrated in Figure 9-2, this is accomplished, in theory, by viewing the space between input and output not as a single black box but as a network of black boxes, each of which represents some particular model or finding about human behavior.

We can construct an example using our previous equation for a straight line. Suppose that we wish to describe performance during an initial period of acquisition, for example, the first five minutes of practice, on some task such as the multiplication tables. Performance during this initial period is a linear function of practice and can be represented as shown in Figure 9-3. Suppose, further, that the function that describes performance versus practice in Figure 9-3 is $R = 2(t) + 3$, where R is some quantifiable aspect of performance such as number of correct responses and t is time or number of practice trials.

Now, by examining performance in this task in various sized groups (such as classrooms) we might discover that working in a group affects performance, but in a uniform way, so that size of group simply changes the value of m from 2 to something else (for instance, for a group consisting of 2 other people m is 5, for a group of 4 other people m is 7 and so forth). What we have discovered is a family of curves, in which the independent variable is amount of practice, and one parameter is the size of the group in which the learner is working. Since the value of m determines the slope of the line, we can say that learning rate appears to be related to size of group. The value of b, the other parameter in our example, is constant and determines where the line in the graph crosses the ordinate. The fact that b is not 0 may indicate that the individuals in our sample knew part of the task at the beginning of the experiment. Our example, although oversimplified, serves to illus-

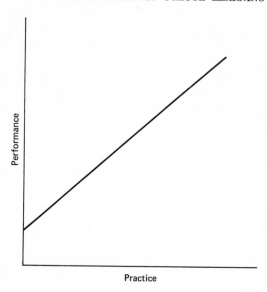

FIGURE 9-3
Performance during the initial five minutes of practice.

trate the difference between parameters and variables and their respective roles in describing behavior.

Description

To formulate hypotheses about the states of a behavioral system as described by Figure 9-2, we draw on existing models for behavior. This is similar to what we did for animal behavior and rote learning in that we are characterizing relationships between independent and dependent variables, rather than generating prescriptive statements for accomplishing behavior change. There is a difference, however, in that now we are attempting to construct mechanisms that account for these relationships by utilizing a variety of models simultaneously. Moreover, it is often the interaction between these models that contributes information about the way in which a given system operates.

As an example, suppose that we want to predict what students will learn about the concept of culture from a one-hour lecture and twenty pages of assigned reading in a textbook. To make the prediction, we might want to know what the students have available in the way of prior knowledge, such as language habits among the words used to define and illustrate the concept in both the lecture and textbook. We can use this information, for instance, to predict proactive interference or facilitation for both acquisition and retention of new material in the lecture and text. Language habits can also give us ideas about similarity and meaningfulness as a basis for predicting transfer effects.

For our prediction to be successful we also need information concerning the empirical characteristics of the discourse used to communicate the concepts. That is, we need information that tells us how words are used in relation to one another both in the textbook and in the lecture. This information can be of value in determining possible sources of both proactive and retroactive interference and facilitation.

In addition to language habits and properties of the discourse, we shall very likely be able to write rules that define terms in the lecture and textbook. These rules can be used to construct particular concept acquisition paradigms (for example, reception versus selection learning). Apart from the above information, we may also want to consider characteristics of students such as interests, age, IQ, sex, and perhaps certain socioeconomic variables. Interactions between variables such as the teacher and student are also relevant.

Another source of empirical and intuitive knowledge concerns strategies of presentation in both lecture and textbook. The questions here are whether material is organized around specific topics or themes, how illustrations are used, the nature of the examples, and so forth. And, finally, we might want information about the time of day the material is presented and whether students have been exposed to considerable information of a similar sort prior to or subsequent to the lecture and textbook reading.

If we expand our original question to include a comparison between two methods 'of instruction (the "methods question" described in Chapter 2), we need to consider the way in which the two sets of verbal materials differ from one another. This also brings into play teacher variables. We need to know, for example, whether the same teacher taught both methods and whether the teacher knew that the method he was using was experimental (a potential Hawthorne effect).

Some of the information needed in order to describe the system used in our example can be obtained from models in the subject matter of psychology (for example, the effect of prior language habits on acquisition and retention and the role of rules in concept acquisition). Additional information can be obtained by talking to teachers and by drawing on the knowledge that curriculum theorists provide about the nature of the subject matter from which the concepts are drawn. When we put such information together in a systematic way and ask about the interaction between the various components (for instance, does the effect of prior language habits depend on the particular set of rules used to define the concepts), we are beginning the kind of systems analysis illustrated in Figure 9-2.

Prescription

Once a behavioral system has been described we can ask about the conditions under which particular states of the system are achieved. This inquiry leads to what we earlier referred to as principles of instruction. From the descriptive statements developed for a system we can construct rules that specify how its independent variables and collective parameters can be arranged so as to achieve whatever outcome we want. The desired state of a system in school learning is not, however, specified by a theory of instruction. It must rather be specified by outside criteria—our "philosophy of education."

The development of principles of instruction is an ultimate goal of the psychology of school learning. As mentioned earlier, however, intuitive prescriptive principles (principles of practice) are often developed and used with considerable success. In fact, intuition can be incorporated into the formulation of descriptive statements on which the principles of instruction are based.

One means of conceptualizing how intuition and systematic experimentation can be used to obtain desired outcomes for instruction is represented in Figure 9-4. Here we see illustrated, schematically, what we shall call the "path of scientific knowledge." This path is nothing more than a way of characterizing our knowledge of the basic variables and parameters of a system from which we predict relationships between stimuli and responses. However, because experimentation within science can seldom take account of all the conditions that operate in a particular situation, we must use our intuition to get from the results of experimentation to the goals of instruction.

In other words, on the basis of scientific knowledge, we make a prediction to a certain domain of behavior within which lies the particular outcome that our instruction is designed to achieve. In lieu of a precise principle of instruction that specifies how we translate our prediction based on scientific knowledge into an instructional outcome, we use informed intuition. Such intuition is simply a personal knowledge of the parameters and variables in a given situation. The teacher, the parent, and the counselor often have such knowledge of human behavior.

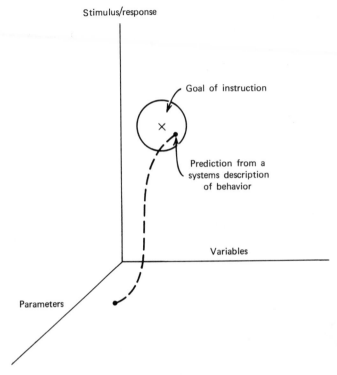

FIGURE 9-4

"The path to scientific knowledge."

And, although this knowledge is not systematically represented and moreover, may not even be at the conscious level of awareness, it can be utilized in transforming the findings of science into practice.

Action Research

Action research is a technique for decision making; it is a way of bringing together information to study a particular situation so that a desired outcome can be achieved. The term also reflects a particular set of procedures for transforming scientific knowledge into practical application. These procedures begin with the systematic observation and manipulation of behavior in natural settings. This observation and manipulation can be accomplished informally by the psychologist, teacher, or parent.

In the formal sense, action research refers to a kind of research activity that employs systems analysis in order to achieve a balanced understanding of real problems. We use this analysis to identify an ensemble (collection) of interacting phenomena where the important characteristics of events are associated with their interactions. Whether we base our understanding of these interactions on a knowledge of psychology or on our prescientific models for behavior is in a sense unimportant. To be sure, we have taken the view that it is more efficient to use models from psychology for many of these interacting elements. At the same time, however, the practitioner can provide much useful information that the psychologist has not yet discovered.

In order to make clear how action research operates, let us define three separate paths to a knowledge of behavior. First, there is a totally experimental path; in this case we base all our knowledge of behavior on experimentation done in the laboratory. This path is the one represented by most of the findings of psychology presented in this book.

Second, we can take a theoretical and analytical path based on idealized (often mathematical) models for behavior. This path has not met with great success in the social sciences although in the natural sciences it has been extremely powerful (for example, mathematical physics).

Third, there is a theoretical and numerical path based on exact models with specific parameters. This third path is represented by simulation of behavioral systems, often with the aid of a computer. Such a path has proven useful in understanding organizational theory and management procedures in business and, to a more limited extent, in understanding certain phenomena in education.

The third path to knowledge is embodied in action research. This can be conceptualized by using the idea of a game. People have developed management games, war games, educational games, and even games of international politics. In each case, a system has been represented in which input conditions are changed and output behaviors are observed. Understanding the rules in such games amounts to learning how the system operates. By taking a complex behavioral system and converting it into a game we can make it amenable to empirical study. Simplifications are, of course, necessary to construct such games, but the resulting understanding of potential variables and parameters usually outweighs what is lost in the conversion.

Every game has two types of rules. There are rules that define acceptable and unacceptable behaviors (moves). These rules must be obeyed if the game is to be played. In addition to rules for playing the game, however, we have a set of rules, often called strategies for playing the game, that optimize certain outcomes such as winning. Thus, in the game of chess, an opening move of pawn to King's Rook—4 is perfectly acceptable, although it would very likely be judged to be a bad move. Pawn to King—4, on the other hand, would be both acceptable and "good."

At this point, some examples of action research applied to behavioral phenomena may be helpful. Let us begin with a simple game such as chess, which we can suppose is constructed to represent the phenomenon of medieval warfare. The various pieces of the game represent the major participants in the phenomenon and the rules for moving the pieces presumably reflect their typical behavior. Because of the way the game is constructed we can study the nature of this type of warfare by having two people play against one another. In addition, however, we could replace one of the players with a computer programmed to play a wide variety of strategies, thus obtaining more information about the behavior of real subjects. Of course, we could also have two computers play against one another, thus exploring an even wider range of alternative strategies for winning.

The point is that, however we choose to study the game, we are able to learn more about the phenomenon it represents than if we were to wait for such warfare to occur or try to arrange for it to occur. Said another way, to study a phenomenon we must be able to manipulate it in some way, and when the phenomenon is real and complex we must often construct an analogy to it in order to accomplish this manipulation. It is also worth noting that we can simulate natural phenomena as well as behavioral phenomena. In this case, however, the result is not a game unless we want to interpret the study of an idealized metal under varying conditions of temperature, stress, and so forth, as a game. The concept of a game arises with regard to behavior because people are involved and because what we want to study is the way they interact with one another.

Another example of a game constructed to study a behavioral system might be called "the game of politics." Suppose that we want to study how an election campaign is structured as a function of the characteristics of an electorate. We can define certain of these characteristics and the "computer voters" who have them; that is, we program a computer so that it contains 500 people with various ethnic, racial, and socioeconomic characteristics. We then tell a group of subjects to structure a campaign—define issues and present them—after which the 500 computer people "vote" for a candidate. By observing the voting behavior of our computer people, we gain potential information about the variables that affect the voting behavior of real people in reaction to actual political campaigns.

Action research can also be employed to study knowledge itself. In this case, we define a subject matter (for example, physics, history, archeology) as a behavioral system. Then we abstract certain features of the system that we use to define the acceptable and unacceptable behaviors of its participants, that is, we define rules according to which the "game" of science is played. Moreover, we must also construct rules for winning; doing physics, but doing it badly, would be a consequence of not complying with these rules. Given the above sets of rules, we can construct a path via simulation to determine how the system works.

We can also extend action research to the classroom. Here, we may want to create a sample of "computer children" with defined characteristics. Various teaching methods and curricula might be presented to the children after which they would be tested for acquisition, understanding, appreciation, or whatever other dependent variables we are interested in and able to quantify.

Games and simulations can be used as instructional devices as well as a means of understanding behavioral phenomena. For example, we might try to teach children about politics by having them perform as subjects in our political campaign game. By observing the results of a campaign structured around a set of defined characteristics, students may gain considerable insight into the actual political process.

The use of games as instructional devices offers fascinating possibilities for the intuitive optimization of instruction. Although their effectiveness is often difficult to evaluate, a frequent reaction from those who employ games in instruction is that children learn many important things from a game that could be taught in no other way except by real life experience. Despite their intuitive appeal, however, we need to develop systematic procedures for measuring acquisition, transfer, and retention of what games are designed to teach.

Summary

Using techniques such as those discussed in Chapters 2–8, we can achieve certain understandings of behavioral phenomena. These understandings are limited, however, by our ability to represent in a laboratory setting the things we are interested in studying. Alternatively, we can attempt a purely theoretical formulation of the problem of interest. But here we are limited by our lack of precise knowledge of the mathematical form of the phenomenon. Thus, we arrive at a third means of studying behavior by which we attempt to (1) create a model and then (2) study the behavior of the model under a wide variety of real life conditions.

The last two approaches enable us to achieve an understanding of behavior in terms of idealized or abstracted properties of the behaving organism. In order to gain a true understanding of human behavior, however, we must use the first approach. For it is on the basis of systematic experimentation with real people that our laws of behavior must ultimately be founded.

Because our present scientific understanding of human behavior is limited does not mean that we as practitioners can afford to ignore it. And because practical decisions about behavioral change are often not grounded in scientific knowledge does not mean that we should ignore their potential relevance for the scientific study of behavior. What we must continue to keep in perspective is the difference between the goal of science and the goal of practice, and how the two can mutually serve one another.

Suggested Readings

Bruner, J. (Ed.) *Learning About Learning: A Conference Report.* U.S. Department of Health, Education and Welfare. 1966. A book of conference papers containing research and theory on both the affective and cognitive dimensions of behavior. The working papers in Appendix A by Roger Brown, Jerome Bruner, and Patrick Suppes are among the best in the book.

Bruner, J. *Toward a Theory of Instruction.* Harvard University Press. 1966. A skillful collection of essays. Almost everyone can find something here of value. The essay entitled "Notes on a Theory of Instruction" is directly relevant to many ideas in this chapter.

DeGroot, A. *Thought and Choice in Chess.* Basic Books Inc. 1965. An example of a massive effort to attack one case of human information processing. For those interested in chess, the book is a must. Others will probably find Chapters 2 and 9 sufficient.

Gagne, R. M. *The Conditions of Learning.* Holt, Rinehart and Winston. 1965. A view of the learning situation in terms of hierarchical behaviors. Gagne is one of the pioneers in the field of modern educational psychology, and the book is meant to be an introductory text. Chapters 9 and 10 on educational systems are relevant for our purposes.

Hilgard, E. R. & Bower, G. H. *Theories of Learning.* Appleton-Century-Crofts. 1966. Chapter 12 by Bower and Chapter 16 by Hilgard are relevant to the system analysis problem discussed in this chapter.

Krumboltz, J. D. *Learning and the Educational Process.* Rand McNally and Co. 1965. Another book of conference papers. Chapter 1 by Gagne on objectives, Chapter 2 by Atkinson on motivation, Chapter 3 by Berlyne on curiosity, and Chapter 8 by Rothkopf on written instruction contain valuable ideas which, while in most cases not new, are well stated.

Kuethe, J. L. *The Teaching-Learning Process.* Scott, Foresmann and Co. 1968. A text written from the point of view of a "discipline of education." Chapter 2 gives the basic arguments as well as examples for application.

Miller, G., Galanter, E., & Pribram, K. *Plans and the Structure of Behavior.* Henry Holt and Co. 1960. One of the landmark texts in modern criticism of associationism. For our purposes, the book illustrates a computer model for analyzing "simplified" behavioral problems. Chapter 3 on simulation is particularly relevant.

Shulman, L. & Keislar, E. (Eds.) *Learning by Discovery.* Rand McNally and Co. 1966. A book of conference papers on one of the perennial problems in education. Although in most papers the problem is avoided as often as it is confronted, Chapter 4 by Wittrock and Chapter 5 by Cronbach are valuable.

Smith, K. & Smith, M. *Cybernetic Principles of Learning and Educational Design.* Holt, Rinehart and Winston, 1966. The systems analysis approach applied to problems in education. The book is introductory in nature with a chapter on almost every aspect of modern educational theory and technology. Chapters 1, 14 and 18 contain the basic points.

Snyder, H. I. *Contemporary Educational Psychology: Some Models Applied to the School Setting.* John Wiley and Sons. 1968. A monograph on the application of mathematical models of behavior to school learning. Much of the material is technical and requires some background or considerable perseverance. Part II on simulation is excellent, particularly Chapter 10.

Westcott, M. R. *Toward a Contemporary Psychology of Intuition.* Holt, Rinehart and Winston. 1968. A modern treatment of a very old problem in psychology. Each chapter has a particular focus, varying from philosophical background to present day research findings. Chapter 2 gives the general psychological basis for the concept of intuition.

Index